未知
風彈奏湖面
曲譜無痕
葉子翻飛飄落
舞姿無迹
讓生命路轉溪橋
讓生活柳暗花明

未曾
青花非花
青衣非衣

像非象
水因勢賦形
欲空則空
欲寂則寂

未竟
一張木椅
有時光的體溫與脈搏
故事在年輪間坐著
閉上眼
你就能瞥見雲起花開
滿山美麗

未
美物近心，溫暖未來

A New Wave of Creativity

CONTEMPORARY CHINESE FURNITURE DESIGN

LAURENCE KING

Published in 2019 by
Laurence King Publishing Ltd
361–373 City Road
London EC1V 1LR
enquiries@laurenceking.com
www.laurenceking.com

Text by Charlotte and Peter Fiell

This publication was developed in partnership
with the China National Furniture Association
and UBM Sinoexpo Ltd.

This work was designed and produced by
Laurence King Publishing Ltd, London.

A catalogue record for this book is
available from the British Library

ISBN: 978-1-78627-492-2

Senior Editor: Andrew Roff
Designer: Alexandre Coco

Printed in China

Laurence King Publishing is committed
to ethical and sustainable production. We are
proud participants in The Book Chain Project®
bookchainproject.com

FRONT ENDPAPER ILLUSTRATION:
CALLIGRAPHIC POSTER
by Hong Wei featuring his Pin Yi chair, 2017

BACK ENDPAPER ILLUSTRATION:
CALLIGRAPHIC POSTER
by Hong Wei featuring his Xi armchair, 2017

→
OBJECT # SQN1-F2 A CHAIR
by Zhang Zhoujie (self-production)
and early computer-generated program,
2011 (pages 214)

PAGE 4
MULAN CHAIR
by in-house design team for
shiershiman, 2018 (page 150)

A New Wave of Creativity

CONTEMPORARY CHINESE FURNITURE DESIGN

Charlotte & Peter Fiell, with Zheng Qu

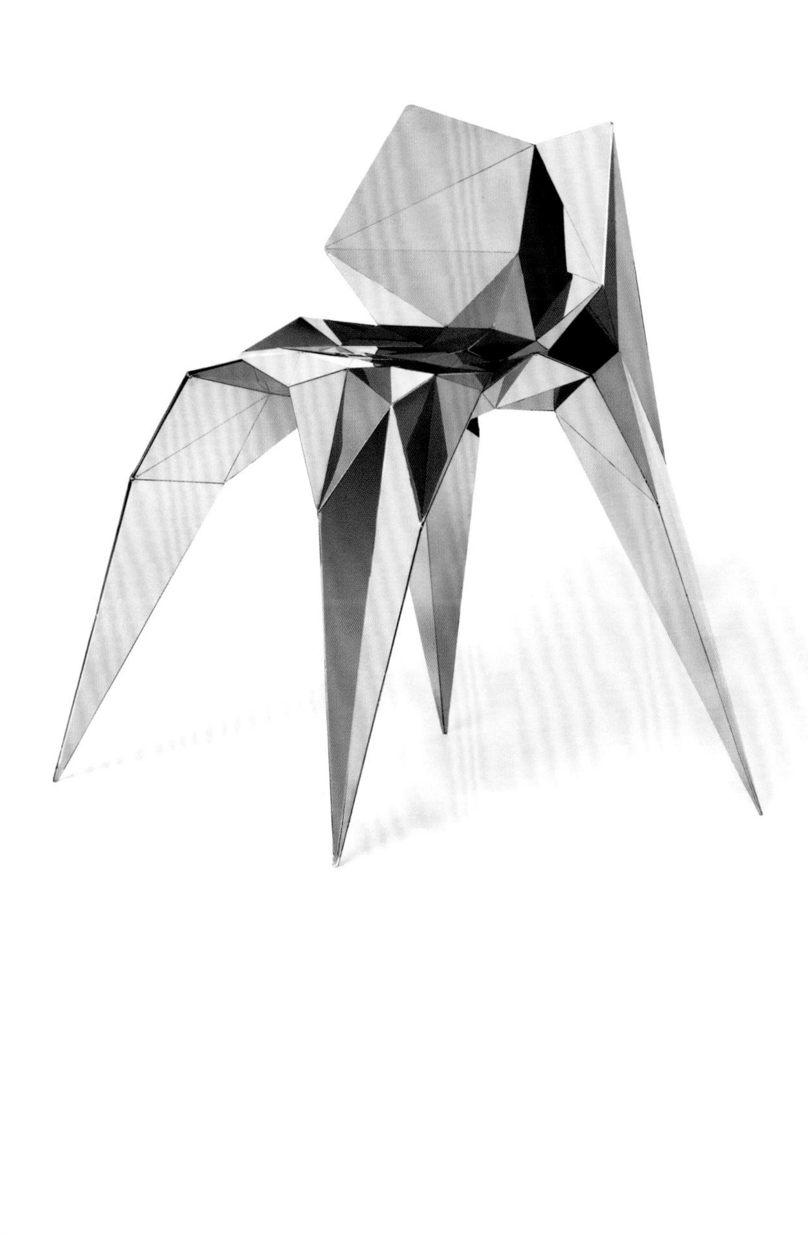

Laurence King Publishing

CONTENTS

THE CREATORS

PREFACE

The publication of this book marks the twenty-fifth anniversary of the Furniture China expo. Held annually in Pudong, Shanghai, every September, the exhibition has gone from strength to strength, and in 2019 takes place in a huge space – 350,000 square metres (the area of 50 football pitches) – and accommodates an impressive variety of new furniture products from 3,500 exhibitors. It also sees the launch of this book, the first by internationally renowned authors to comprehensively survey contemporary Chinese furniture design. It features over 400 exemplary works, every one of them representative of the new wave of creativity in modern Chinese furniture design.

Our first meeting with authors Charlotte and Peter Fiell convinced us that they shared our aim of introducing a global audience to the extraordinary creativity and originality in contemporary Chinese furniture design, and they subsequently made a special trip to Furniture China expo in order to select representative designs for the book. As you will see, they have also included examples of outstanding furniture from previous expos, as well as signature works recommended by various designers they visited during their research trip.

We hope that the publication of this book will excite the world's interest in Chinese furniture and stimulate a desire for even more knowledge about it. Today there are some 60,000 furniture manufacturers operating in China, and over 100,000 designers contribute directly or indirectly to the design of furniture. Their products are sold to a home market of about 1.4 billion people, and the annual export value of furniture is roughly $50 billion. It is a hugely buoyant and productive field, and the creativity within China's contemporary furniture design scene is truly astonishing.

China has the largest talent pool in the world, and has produced virtuosos in every area, from sport and music to science, art and design. The designs collected in this book are stylistically diverse, but, perhaps more importantly, each and every one has a refreshing originality, while at the same time reflecting its distinctively Chinese roots.

Over the last decade Furniture China expo has been dedicated to promoting original Chinese furniture design and has built innumerable 'show stages' for both designers and brands. Our Brand Design Hall and Design of Designers (DOD) events have acted as platforms for the emergence of numerous new stars of the industry. Last year, we launched yet another event, Creation of Creators (COC), which aims to empower the Chinese furniture industry from a more diversified perspective.

As for the coming decade, Furniture China, along with new waves of creativity and 5,000 years of cultural tradition, will continue driving innovation in China's fast-developing furniture industry. We hope this inspirational book will act as a catalyst, pushing creativity in China's furniture industry to even more exciting heights.

GÙ BAMBOO PAPER CHAIR
by Pinwu (self-production), 2012
– originally created for the craft-inspired
'From Yuhang' project

Xu Xiangnan
President of China National
Furniture Association (CNFA)

Wang Mingliang
Founder of Shanghai UBM Sinoexpo
International Exhibition Co.

FOREWORD

This foreword is written against a background that sees the first China International Import Expo (CIIE) being staged in Shanghai, while trade friction between China and the United States escalates. It is also a time when China's domestic economic progress is slowing down for the first time after uninterrupted, decades-long growth. The rampant-growth development model is gradually abating, and Chinese consumer habits are changing too. Boastfulness is being replaced with greater rationalism, indigenous Chinese products are becoming increasingly popular, and homegrown brands incorporating both tradition and sustainability are on the rise. However, the extent of Chinese consumption – an extraordinary ¥213.5 billion ($26.6 billion) in just one day on Tmall, the Chinese equivalent of Amazon – has shocked many people and caused much controversy within this vast Asian furniture-producing country. A common reaction has been, 'This is China,' but that statement can convey a whole range of emotions – anything from dismay, astonishment and confusion, to disbelief, anger and jealousy. No matter how you take it, 'This is China' describes the country today, and this era is the one that has given birth to contemporary Chinese design.

In my opinion, the evolution of furniture design results from countless micro-innovations in fields ranging from material science to cultural heritage. These can be seen as the drivers behind the survival (and promotion) of good design. Look at China's culture of extreme minimalism, as represented by Ruyao ware – a rare variety of ceramics from the Song dynasty. This is complemented by the free-hand brushwork of the Yuan dynasty, which painted vivid scenes with just a few strokes, and the restrained elegance of furniture from the Ming dynasty. All these elements are embodied in the literati aesthetic, the style associated with scholarly pursuits and that imposed moral restrictions on materials. In his famous book *Treatise on Superfluous Things*, Wen Zhenheng, writing during the Ming dynasty, records the Chinese literati's graceful interests and refined taste, specifications for objects and furniture, and their aesthetic principles. It was modestly called a book of 'useless things' by the author, but in fact outlines everything that the literati pursued in their quest for a spiritual life.

All these cultural 'genes' have an enduring history, whether in explicit or implicit forms. The development of China's furniture design in the last two decades is obviously an explicit process. The process of integrating traditional culture and contemporary style in furniture was initiated by designers such as Zhu Xiaojie, Chi Wing Lo, Chen Renyi, Shao Fan, Shi Jianmin and Song Tao, but many others have since joined the movement, notably Lv Yongzhong, Lydon Neri, Rossana Hu, Jiang Qiong'er, Jeff Shi Dayu, Wen Hao, Shen Baohong, Studio MVW, Chen Darui, Zhong Song, Chen Yanfei and Jerry Chen. The style they pursue has grown from being virtually unknown a decade ago, to becoming the one that is most favoured by the market. Thus the term 'New Chinese Style' came into being. Although the quality and taste within that style varies considerably, it is a definable phenomenon that demonstrates a growing recognition of native culture by the general public. In addition, brands that were born and grown online, such as Ziinlife, Bentu, MZGF and E-Y Products™, are also supporters of Chinese-inspired design. Indeed, the rediscovery and recognition of traditional Chinese design culture has been the single most important factor within

the development of the Chinese furniture industry over the past 20 years, in which native Chinese designers have played a crucial role.

Inevitably, changes brought about by rapid development can lead to social problems, as has been happening in China. The artist Liu Xiaodong once said, 'I do not paint for the purpose of creating a perfect picture, but for the hope of seeing more social engagement and awareness. I know deep down in my heart about the powerlessness of the arts in changing and influencing ... society, but it has truly made me feel the pain of living.' His brutally realistic artworks comment on such things as the controversial Three Gorges dam, the outbreak of the SARS virus and the growing problem of smog, and all project a vivid picture of a cold and hard reality.

While design in China continues to be dominated by the 'trendy bestsellers' model, so design for the 'common good' becomes increasingly rare. All actions are connected to some kind of outcome, and the revenue-driven mindset has built a pathway for counterfeiting. Within this context, 'Design' (with a capital D) needs to focus on how best to deliver goodness and arouse thoughtfulness. Some practitioners have already emerged in this area, including Echo Publishing, which for the past four decades has devoted itself to seeking and collecting all kinds of traditional Chinese folk items; the ten Chinese interior designers who initiated C Foundation in 2014 with the aim of nurturing society through design; and the Rong Design Library in Hangzhou, which has been gathering information on folk techniques and skills, and using them in real terms.

Given its vast size, large population and highly variable regional development, China is in pressing need of design-driven upgrades. This is especially true for the more disadvantaged members of Chinese society. They too deserve life-enhancing design, and their needs deserve special attention and actions from all designers.

In the words of the economist Xu Xiaonian, 'the decline of macro-level economic development during the bottleneck period of [today's] China actually leaves room for the micro-level. Innovation is key for this era.' Apart from physical innovations, such as technology and form, there are also innovations on the psychological level. If the innovation of technology could be interpreted in ancient Chinese philosophical terms as gaining knowledge through the study of things, then psychological innovation is equal to the traditional idea of cultivating a righteous heart with good virtue; or, to put it another way, it can alter people's value systems and aesthetic taste.

The concept of 'less is more' was popularized 90 years ago by the German-American architect Ludwig Mies van der Rohe, but is still applicable today. After four decades of economic growth, China has entered a stage of overproduction, which encourages unlimited desire, spoils people with too much choice, and creates a situation where 'more' has become negative.

An era that promotes 'less' is due to arrive in China, and in my opinion is the natural result of dramatic economic progress that influences people both physically and psychologically. To consume less or ask for less is not intrinsically negative; rather, it is about designing, producing and using in a more considerate way. A piece of furniture, for example, could be merely fanciful, but it could also be used as a tool for self-cultivation. Furthermore, producing fewer fanciful designs could lead to higher quality in what is produced. In the opinion of the German industrial designer Dieter Rams, 'Good design is long-lasting. It avoids being fashionable and therefore never appears antiquated. Unlike fashionable design, it lasts many years – even in today's throwaway society ... Good design is environmentally friendly'. Designers should consider the necessity of a design. Why should there be a new design? Is it to meet new demands? Does this new demand truly exist, or is it just self-deception? These questions must be answered with supporting evidence, or else designers will simply be producing more rubbish in different forms. This new and much-needed mindset recalls the teaching of Laozi 2,000 years ago, when he observed, 'to have little is to have more; to have much is to be confused'. This urges us to rethink our own clouded circumstances.

The concept of 'design for the real world', praised so highly by the Chinese design researcher Liu Guanzhong, was first proposed by the Austrian designer Victor Papanek in the 1970s. He advocated design that was both socially and ecologically responsible, a debate that is highly relevant to what China is going through today. As he noted of the Western consumer-driven societies, 'The cancerous growth of the creative individual expressing himself egocentrically at the expense of spectators and/or consumer has spread from the arts, overrun most of the crafts, and finally reached into design. No longer does the artist, craftsman, or in some cases the designer operate with the good of the consumer in mind; rather, many creative statements have become highly individualistic, auto-therapeutic little comments by the artist to himself.'

Thankfully, change is underway. It can be seen in the Ming Xuan Garden built in New York's Metropolitan Museum by the Chinese architect Chen Congzhou some 40 years ago, and in the more recent design of the Lucas Museum of Narrative Art by Ma Yansong. It is also evident in Wang Shixiang's authoritative book *The Connoisseurship of Chinese Furniture: Ming and Early Qing Dynasties* (1990), and in the promotion of parametricism by the digital artist and designer Zhang Zhoujie. All these developments show that Chinese design has begun to respond to and interact with the rest of the world. It is a pleasure to see this change, for it means that we have finally joined the arena of international design. However, there is still a long way to go before we become a recognized arbiter.

I first met Charlotte and Peter Fiell, the authors of this book, in 2017. They are widely recognized by the international community for their professional design publications based on substantial interviews and in-depth investigations. As a member of the contemporary Chinese design community, I look forward to their considered analysis as international commentators of this remarkable era in Chinese design.

Hou Zheng-Guang
Vice-director of Design Committee of China Furniture Association; Vice-director of Shanghai Industrial Design Association; Founder of MoreLess Furniture

INTRODUCTION

LEARNING FROM THE PAST AND LOOKING TO THE FUTURE

Since the mid-1990s a definable movement in contemporary Chinese furniture design has been growing and evolving, and has now reached such creative critical mass that it is possible to speak of it enjoying a 'moment'. The publication of this book is intended to share this remarkable design story with the wider world, while introducing the work and ideas of its leading protagonists. The exceptional quality and innovation of the furniture associated with what has already become known as 'New Chinese Design' will undoubtedly set in motion a significant reappraisal of contemporary Chinese design in general. But what is more, this extraordinary development may initiate the tipping of the balance of international design influence from West to East, such is its astonishing creative vitality and snowballing momentum.

The first thing to understand about New Chinese Design is that it is foremost a design reform movement. Ideologically guided, it has been responsible for an extraordinary renaissance within Chinese furniture design, the first green shoots of which began to emerge in isolation with the designs of Samuel Chan in Britain during the late 1980s. It then coalesced into a definable movement in mainland China in the mid-1990s with the work of artist-designers such as Shao Fan, Song Tao and the late Chen Zhen, as well as the craftsman-designer Zhu Xiaojie. The movement's momentum has steadily built over the intervening two-and-a-half decades, with successive generations of talented Chinese designers tapping into their cultural roots in order to create original and innovative furniture pieces that are inspired by the remarkable design legacy of their ancient forebears. Channelling the spirit of the Song and Ming dynasties, as well as other Chinese styles and themes, these designs express a twenty-first-century Sinocentric national romanticism. And in our increasingly globalized world, the focus on cultural roots is becoming ever more important, for they have the power to reconnect us with where we come from and help give us a sense of who we are, our place in the world, and ultimately our shared humanity. By drawing inspiration from their 5,000-year-old culture, today's Chinese designers are able to imbue their work with an all-important sense of identity or character, and that is what people are responding to on a deep emotional level. In other words, the cultural rooting of design can provide 'the feel' that makes contextualizing sense of form and function.

More than this, the New Chinese Design phenomenon has also opened up an important debate among Chinese designers and design educators about the ultimate goals and ethics of design, as Mr Hou so eloquently articulates in the foreword to this book. This new focus on defining what good design is and why its adoption is so imperative for China will undoubtedly produce major benefits both nationally and internationally. That is because the level of thoughtfulness underlying any design thinking ultimately determines the inherent value of what is produced and consumed. It has, therefore, far-reaching social, economic and environmental implications. Certainly, the sands of consciousness are rapidly shifting within Chinese design circles, and that is without question a hugely encouraging development. Today, in our increasingly interconnected world, what happens in China in terms of design and manufacturing has an impact not only within its borders, but elsewhere, too. Given this, thankfully there is a remarkable level of talent, intelligence and resourcefulness among the pioneers of New Chinese Design, who, with encouragement and the right conditions, could have a tremendously positive influence on world design. Indeed, within the context of this specific moment in Chinese design, it feels that this is not so much a question of 'if', but rather 'when?'

Detail of an anonymous painting, entitled *Banquet and Concert*, which depicts elegant ladies of the imperial court enjoying a feast and music, while seated on mid-level stools around a mid-level table. Tang dynasty, 10th century

Palace portrait on a hanging scroll of Emperor Taizu (born Zhao Kuangyin), founder of the Song dynasty, who reigned 960–976. National Palace Museum in Taipei

<u>PROJECT NO.1 FROM 2004</u>
by Shao Fan (self-production), 2004

The numbers bear this prediction out, for according to Ralph Wiegmann, the CEO of the iF Design Awards, there are an estimated one million Chinese art and design students studying in China at any one time, and, as he noted in a talk at the 2017 China Craft Week in Hangzhou, 'if only 1 per cent of them are any good then that constitutes more [design] graduates than the whole of Europe combined.' In fact, there are more than 100 art and technical colleges in China that specifically teach furniture design, and each year more than 5,000 students graduate from their courses. And that is not counting the sizeable cohort of students studying abroad, a significant percentage of whom are being trained at the top design teaching institutions in the world. Nor does it include the legions of product designers, interior designers and architects who also inevitably gravitate towards furniture design during their careers. But apart from this incredible pool of creative talent, there is also an interesting synergistic clustering effect taking place among the acknowledged stars of contemporary Chinese furniture design, all of whom are featured over the coming pages. In fact, it is this dynamic synergy, especially between the different generations of designers, that has creatively sustained and ultimately shaped the evolution of New Chinese Design over the last 25 years.

So, how can the term 'New Chinese Design' be best defined? It is a loosely organized groundswell of designers, of Chinese birth or descent, who are looking back to their indigenous design roots for inspiration and creating work that embodies the Chinese cultural spirit in refreshingly contemporary ways. To date, it is in the realm of furniture that New Chinese Design has made the most definable inroads into changing and radically improving the status quo. And while the styles, methods, materials and cultural references that have been used to achieve this are remarkably diverse – as the designs, ranging from the cutting-edge avant-garde to the progressive mainstream, featured in the coming pages reveal – each and every one of these carefully selected pieces of furniture possesses at its core a distinctive Chinese character, sometimes subtly whispered and at other times exuberantly hollered. Given China's rich design history, it might seem strange to those in the West that this has not happened before, given that many design icons of Danish Modernism, for instance, can trace their formal ancestry back to historical Chinese archetypes. Among the most famous examples of this are Hans Wegner's Ming-derived China Chair (1944), Chinese Chair (1945) and Cow-Horn Chair (1952), which are – somewhat ironically – among the most widely copied chair designs in China today.

Certainly, in the West various historic Chinese object typologies have long been seen as instructively representing 'ideal' forms. Yet for much of the twentieth century, China's design past was consigned to the annals of history – with the emphasis being firmly placed on forward-looking

progress. Another reason for this seeming disregard of historic design culture is that it is all too easy to take one's own society for granted when one is immersed in it, and it is only with distance that its core values become more apparent and understandable. In fact, it is no coincidence that the vast majority of designers associated with New Chinese Design gained this valuable perspective on their own culture while studying abroad. Another thing that is quite surprising, at least from a Western standpoint, is that until very recently design teaching syllabuses in China have largely, if not entirely, focused on teaching an established Western canon of design – with Bauhaus Modernism being held up as the shining exemplar. Many of the designers interviewed for this book related how they learned about the rich design culture of the Song and Ming dynasties by conducting their own self-guided research. And the more they learned from collecting antiques, rooting out specialist publications or visiting museum collections, the more enthralled they became with this seemingly 'lost' design legacy. Their inquiries not surprisingly uncovered a wonderful fount of design inspiration, from elegant Ming forms and ancient symbolic motifs to precisely executed mortise and tenon joinery and long-forgotten lacquering techniques. But even more importantly, through this research they rediscovered the refined aestheticism and lifestyle culture of the Chinese literati, based on the ethical humanism of Confucianism, which represents an alternative mode of being that is the very antithesis of the unbridled consumerism that has been such a defining factor of globalization over the last thirty years – and, of course, China's own economic miracle.

In fact, the recent history of China's furniture industry reflects the extraordinary growth unleashed by Deng Xiaoping's introduction of landmark economic reforms and open-door policies in December 1978. As Professor Xu Mei Qi, a leading furniture historian, explained to us, 'over the last thirty years or so, Chinese furniture went from being a very small industry to becoming one of the largest, and today it represents a 1,300 billion yuan annual output, among which approximately 30 per cent was exported.' And while much of that revenue stems from Chinese companies producing furniture for overseas brands, throughout the last decade a significant number of home-grown start-ups have appeared, creating original New Chinese Style furniture for the burgeoning domestic market. Some of the more outward-looking of these so-called design brands have already made inroads into export markets, and the success of these daring design entrepreneurs has woken up larger and more established Chinese furniture manufacturers to the fact that true authenticity and originality can actually make the best business sense.

One of the thorniest issues facing China's current furniture industry is the use of rosewood. Growing demand, especially among home-market consumers, has over recent years far outstripped sustainable supply. In 2016 John Scanlon, the Secretary General of CITES (Convention on International Trade in Endangered Species of Wild Fauna and Flora), highlighted the fact that the survival of 300 different species of prized tropical hardwoods is now under threat. That same year, to legally protect this dwindling supply, over 250 species were added to the international treaty that regulates the tropical hardwood trade through logging permits and agreed quotas, to which China is a very important signatory. Sadly, however, illegal trafficking of exotic woods is still a major problem, and accounts for an estimated 50 to 90 per cent of the hardwoods harvested in Amazonia, Central Africa and Southeast Asia. Not only does illegal logging jeopardise the on-going survival of certain wood species, but it is also leading to the pointless destruction of important natural habitats, which are home to some of the world's most endangered animals. Moreover, illegal logging is also contributing to climate-altering deforestation.

Thankfully, however, growing environmental awareness in China is already leading to a shift in attitudes and tastes, especially among the younger generation. Certainly, it is a difficult dilemma to resolve because the use of these rare tropical hardwoods is so inextricably bound, through the threads of time, to China's extraordinary historic furniture culture. That said, a significant proportion of Chinese manufacturers are already eschewing rosewood in favour of sustainably harvested American walnut, which has a similar grain and colour. This is a trend that will hopefully continue to grow, and which crucially allows Chinese manufacturers the possibility of exporting to important overseas markets, such as the USA and Europe, where the importation of rosewood furniture is so tightly regulated that it is effectively banned.

Against the background of today's Chinese furniture industry, it is perhaps instructive to delve into the long yet fascinating history of Chinese furniture design in order to understand why it is having such a formative influence on the work of contemporary Chinese designers. With thousands of years of continuous history, the story of China has been marked by cycles of chaos and order. Unsurprisingly, it is those periods marked by social stability and prosperity that have witnessed the greatest cultural highpoints in Chinese design. For centuries, however, the Chinese had a mat culture, so what little furniture was produced tended to be low level. The earliest surviving example of this type of furniture, according to the historian Zhang Xiaoming in her book *Chinese Furniture: Exploring China's Furniture Culture* (2009), is a 4,000-year-old small painted wooden table, which was unearthed during excavations at the Neolithic settlement of Taosi in Shanxi province in 1978. Some excavated bronze sacrificial vessels from the Shang (c. 16th–11th centuries BC) and Western Zhou (c. 11th century–771 BC) dynasties are also considered to be very early surviving examples of Chinese furniture, because they had add-on parts that enabled them to be adapted in order to also function as tables for animal sacrifices and the display of wine.

It was during the Zhou dynasty that improved iron-making techniques were introduced, enabling the manufacture of higher-quality tools, which in turn made the production of wooden furniture easier. Indeed, the legendary Zhou engineer-inventor and master craftsman Lu Ban is famously regarded as the father of Chinese carpentry, having reputedly invented the saw, the drill, the plane, the carpenter's square and the carpenter's sink marker. Crucially, it was these types

of better-performing tool that heralded the introduction of innovative tenon-based joinery techniques, which would become such a defining feature of Chinese furniture from the later Song (AD 906–1279) and Ming (AD 1368–1644) dynasties. Lacquered low-level furniture items were also produced, with examples from the Chu state (8th century BC) displaying a remarkable level of technical sophistication and aesthetic artistry given their date. It was also during the Zhou dynasty, as well as the overlapping Warring States period (403–221 BC) and the later Qin dynasty (221–206 BC), that a veritable design and mass-manufacturing revolution took place in China, with a number of highly advanced concepts being introduced and perfected for the very first time, most notably component standardization and interchangeability together with quality-control systems. These powerful ideas heralded what we now think of as 'modern' industrialized production, yet this was some 2,500 years earlier than these same concepts were developed in the West, showing just how incredibly advanced Chinese design and manufacture were at this stage. That said, in terms of furniture design, the custom was still to kneel or sit cross-legged on woven mats or use propping armrests while lying in a semi-recumbent position. As a consequence, low tables and screens were really the only 'proper' furniture items produced, with the latter being used to delineate living spaces.

Chinese furnishing habits, however, changed markedly during the succeeding Han dynasty (202 BC–8 AD + AD 25–200). Spanning four centuries, the Han

represented China's first golden age of creative endeavour thanks to unprecedented prosperity brought about by the establishment of the vast trading network we now know as the Silk Road. The exposure to foreign influences that this brought about, the fusion of the ethnic cultures within China's borders and the migration of Buddhism from India ultimately began changing furnishing tastes during this period. It was also during the Han dynasty that a new embossing technique for lacquerwork was developed for furniture, while raised bed-like platforms and low couches began to be used by high-ranking officials and religious dignitaries. These designs had a two-fold function in that they not only raised the sitter off cold earth floors, but also symbolized their elevated social status. Low tray-like tables and folding *huchang* stools, as used by the nomadic 'barbarians' of the northern and western regions, also became popular, as did hourglass-shaped stools constructed of woven straw or rattan.

These different so-called dwarf furniture pieces can be seen as transitional designs that effectively bridged the gap between the woven mats of earlier times and later 'high' furniture, meaning stools and chairs that allowed one's legs to drop down, as well as height-matched tables. The use of these more advanced furniture items became commonplace among the elite classes during the ensuing Tang dynasty (AD 618–907). It was at this time that, as Zhang Xiaoming explains, 'Chinese furniture developed systematically and could be divided into the following types: furniture for sitting and lying, for support and placing other articles, for storage and bracket-type furniture.'

YOKE-BACK ARMCHAIR
Ming dynasty, 16th century.
Philadelphia Museum of Art – this 'Guanmaoshiyi' chair is made of *huanghuali* rosewood, highly prized for its shimmering grain

ARMCHAIR
Qing dynasty, late 18th/early 19th century.
Philadelphia Museum of Art – made from *zitan* (a dark-hued rosewood) and features painstakingly carved relief decoration

Paintings from this period reveal a significant level of furnishing sophistication, with chairs, tables and stools being used that are not so dissimilar from what we use today – albeit they were set at a rather curious mid-height. Nevertheless, throughout the Tang dynasty, Chinese furniture styles continued to mature and evolve, and ultimately laid many of the design foundations for the furniture of the subsequent Song dynasty.

The Song dynasty was an astonishing golden age in Chinese history, especially when compared to the chaotic period that preceded it, when rival warlords had broken the country up into various competing fiefdoms. Divided into two distinct periods, the Northern Song (AD 960–1127) and the Southern Song (AD 1127–1279), it was an era distinguished, for the most part, by political stability and social civility, as well as remarkable technological innovation and scientific advancement. During the reign of the Emperor Taizu, a general who had reunified much of China and was the Song dynasty's founder, the provincial backwater of Kaifeng was transformed into the most exciting city on earth thanks to enlightened governance. The 'City of Memory', as it later became known, boasted a population of over a million people, and because there were no curfews imposed, unlike in other towns and cities, restaurants, music, poetry and painting all thrived. It was also during the Song dynasty that the concept of 'the weekend' was first introduced. This new leisure time encouraged the pursuit of all kinds of activities and pleasures. China's most renowned artwork, *Along the River During the Qingming Festival*, painted by Zhang Zeduan in the early twelfth century, vividly captures the daily life of ordinary people living in Kaifeng, and opens a captivating window on to the world's very first lifestyle culture.

The influence of Confucianism during the Song dynasty also spawned an educational revolution, with new schools of learning and academies giving rise to a new stratum of society: the literati. These scholar-officials, on passing a three-tiered imperial civil examination known as *jinshi*, were recruited as bureaucrats to work in government. The Confucian syllabus they studied for these tough degree-like exams was essentially humanist in emphasis, stressing humility, duty, virtue and morality. In fact, the literati ethos of learning and good character pervaded the very fabric of the Song's new meritocratic society, as well as the design of its furniture. In terms of chairs, their seat and back heights were significantly elevated during this period to what would now be considered as 'normal' chair proportions, while back rails started to furl characteristically inwards. By this stage, chairs and tables were becoming commonplace in the homes of high-ranking officials, and various new chair forms began appearing, including the *Taishi* (Prince Teacher's) with its characteristic top rail acting as a supporting headrest. The use of mortise and tenon joinery also became more widespread, and because of this, furniture from this era tended to have a much greater degree of formal refinement than had previously been achieved.

During the Song dynasty traditional post-and-beam framing techniques were borrowed from architecture and applied to the construction of furniture, thereby establishing an important design blueprint for subsequent Chinese case furniture pieces. Numerous other well-known decorative devices and functional elements relating to furniture were invented during the Song, including cabriole legs, waisted-corner legs and horse-hoof feet. Most Song furniture was characterized by an elegant simplicity, however. Very few examples have survived because they were invariably made from softer local woods, and so were susceptible to rot and woodworm. Today's Chinese furniture designers are more inspired by the lifestyle concepts that were introduced in the Song dynasty than by Song furniture per se.

During the short-lived Mongol-led Yuan dynasty (AD 1271–1368), which bridged the gap between the Song and the

SHELVED CABINET (one of a pair) Republican Period, c. 1920s. Philadelphia Museum of Art – this Sino-Art Deco 'Shugui' (shelved cabinet) is made from *huanghuali* rosewood and incorporates a distinctively Chinese circular brass locking plate and matching hinges

CURVE CHAIR by Samuel Chan (self-production), 1987 – this landmark New Chinese design was first exhibited at the Fiell Gallery in New King's Road, London, in 1988; its form is based on the Chinese character for 'girl'

Ming, furniture tended to be rather grandiose and was often heavily lacquered and embellished with painted decoration to provide smooth glass-like surfaces that were unattainable using wood alone. In fact, the Yuan dynasty's only real invention of note in terms of furniture design was the introduction of drawers. In contrast, the Ming dynasty marked the real highpoint in the development of classical Chinese furniture. The Ming – which means 'bringer of light' – was founded by Hongwu, a mighty rebel peasant-warrior who had forced the Mongols to retreat and had then claimed the imperial Mandate of Heaven. This ruthless emperor was also a genius strategist who presided over one of China's most dazzling eras, which was marked by strong government, social stability and high civilization. Under his rule, a new mercantile spirit was encouraged, which saw the opening up of ever more trade routes and, as a consequence, rising prosperity. As people grew wealthier, they wanted to acquire better and more fashionable furniture.

The cabinet-making boom that occurred during the Ming dynasty can be attributed to three main factors: the preservation of artisanal furniture-making skills that had been passed down to Ming craftsmen; increased ocean-going commerce, which led to greater levels of disposable income; and the lifting in 1567 of a ban that resulted in vast quantities of tropical hardwoods being imported into China from Southeast Asia, significantly bolstering the availability of these prized timbers. In terms of its design, Ming furniture was epitomized by a pared-down, almost proto-modern formal simplicity that relied on perfect proportions, beautifully matched woods, exquisite seamless joinery, smooth unadorned surfaces, elegant flowing lines and minimal ornamentation.

This sophisticated yet understated furniture, though reflecting the rarefied tastes of the literati, also became popular among the newly wealthy mercantile classes. During the Ming period, nouveau riche wealth gave rise to conspicuous consumption, which prompted the increased production of fine furniture. In Ming furniture the natural beauty of the wood grain was emphasized, with rare rosewoods such as *huanghuali* and *zitan* being especially valued. Sometimes elegant latticework and subtle carving were incorporated into Ming furniture, which accentuated the beauty of its constructional logic. Indeed, it is no surprise that the rediscovery of such

a rich indigenous furniture culture has led today's Chinese designers to seek to interpret it through their own contemporary designs. Their enthralment is very much focused on Ming furniture's inherent DNA – its design, materials and construction.

By the 1630s, cracks had begun appearing in the once seemingly invincible Ming state, which – feeling threatened by overseas influence – began to look inwards and became increasingly autocratic. The financial drain of a war with the Japanese in Korea, various natural disasters from flooding to famine, silk-weaver strikes and peasant rebellions all eventually led to a severe economic breakdown. In a weakened condition, the Ming were unable to repel the Manchus as they swept down from the northeast, thereby ending their 276 years of rule. With this Manchu conquest, the last great Chinese dynasty was born, the Qing (AD 1644–1911), which is regarded, after Ming, as the second most important period for the development of classical Chinese furniture.

Taken as a whole, Qing furniture, in line with its Manchurian ancestry, tended to be larger and more imposing than earlier Ming designs. It also at times featured more elaborate carving and inlaid decoration. Furniture from the Qing era is often classified into three distinct phases: the first (1644–1722) saw the continuation of Ming furniture-making traditions, with designs still possessing simple yet elegant forms; the second (1723–1820) saw furniture becoming larger and increasingly more elaborate, often incorporating several materials and techniques into a single design; the third (1821–1911) witnessed a decline of both craftsmanship and taste, with designs often being encrusted with heavily carved ornamentation, which can be thought of as the Chinese Neo-Revivalist equivalent to the British High Victorian style. As the collector and designer Jerry Chen insightfully noted to us, 'all the dynasties appreciated beauty differently, and their different styles are absolutely associated with the culture of the times'.

The desires and aspirations of Chinese society were likewise mirrored in the furniture designs that came after the Chinese Revolution of 1911, which heralded the birth of modern China. After the overthrow of the last imperial dynasty and the establishment of the Republic of China, a new sense of international modernity briefly blossomed in China under the presidency of Sun Yat-sen, which saw

Shanghai become one of the world's most cosmopolitan cities. Furniture created in the then-fashionable Chinese Art Deco style of the 1920s and 1930s reflected the increasing influence of European taste, yet still managed to retain a distinctive Chinese quality.

But while Shanghai was enjoying its heady Jazz Age, inequality was widening between rich and poor. Famine and disease, especially in rural communities, eventually provoked a peasant-led rebellion against the political status quo, and ultimately brought the rise of the Communist Party, led by Mao Zedong. Although the Nationalists and Communists joined forces during the Japanese invasion of Manchuria in the early 1930s, and remained allies throughout the Second World War, once that conflict ended a bitter civil war ensued. Its eventual cession saw the founding of the People's Republic of China in 1949, which signalled a new chapter in Chinese furniture history. In line with the political doctrine of the time, furniture created from the early 1950s through to the early 1990s was heavily influenced by Soviet design ideals. As a result, form followed no-nonsense function. As the designer Song Tao explained to us, this furniture 'had no emotion, just function', but even so, since the late 1980s this type of furniture from the 1950s, 1960s and 1970s, often referred to as being in the '30 Years' style, has become increasingly collectible, much like the retro furniture from those decades in the West.

Often this utility-style furniture was handmade by people for their own use, utilizing whatever materials they could lay their hands on. In fact, the fabrication of this kind of 'make-do' furniture was seen as a test of prowess for young men, and an indicator of potential marital suitability. Although much of this furniture was handmade, there are a few mass-manufactured seating designs from the period that are regarded as iconic because they were so popular. The most famous of these was the Landbond armchair developed by the Canton Landbond Group in 1992, which is seen to represent a veritable milestone in Chinese furniture design because it infused a modern Chinese sensibility with ergonomic considerations. This armchair's popularity was unprecedented and marked the first time in Chinese furniture history, as its manufacturer explains, that 'a single product occupied the whole market and kept selling out … it could be found in almost every sales place across the country, most of them were imitations.' In fact, it has been estimated that at least 100 million examples of this chair were sold, including counterfeits, and its success was seen to represent a new modern direction for furniture design in China. A later design that is likewise regarded as an important early expression of contemporary modern Chinese design is the Swallow Tail stool designed by Lv Yongzhong in 2005, comprising solid wood elements that lock together like a Chinese puzzle. Like the Landbond chair, it has had innumerable 'homages' paid to it.

Although the first tentative expressions of New Chinese Design were evinced in the work of the British-based designer Samuel Chan as early as the late 1980s, it was the artist Shao Fan's creation of his landmark Chairs(?) art furniture series in 1995 that must be regarded as the incendiary touch paper that set off the whole movement in China. This pioneering design-reform crusade has since evolved and matured into a remarkable force of creativity. The innovative and imaginative works resulting from this exciting two-and-a-half-decade adventure not only mark a new watershed moment within Chinese design, but also will undoubtedly radically alter, around the world, people's perceptions of what 'Made in China' really means today. Even more than this, as a significant collective body of work, New Chinese Design, as showcased in this book, unequivocally testifies to the British historian and broadcaster Michael Wood's belief, as expounded in his BBC *Story of China* documentary series, that the march of modern progress 'means embracing history. For to be open about history, after all, is a foundation of a better present and a better future.' And that is ultimately why so many Chinese designers today are looking back in order to look forward. Perhaps this is not so surprising, for it was the Chinese philosopher Confucius who said 2,500 years ago: 'Study the past, if you would divine the future.'

SWALLOW TAIL STOOL
by Lv Yongzhong for Banmoo, 2005

SUMMER PALACE 2 CONSOLE TABLE
by July Chow (self-production), 2012

KHORA COLLECTION
by Adrian Cheng + Shigeru Uchida,
2016–17 (pages 56–7)

THE CREATORS

BENTU

CONCRETE DESIGN

Bentu was founded by Xu Gang in 2011. More than anything, the firm is focused on the design potential of materials left over by the building and ceramic industries, namely cement, stone aggregate, waste aggregate, shattered ceramics and glass. Bentu recycles these by-products to make innovative composite materials, including a kind of terrazzo, as well as an eco-friendly high-strength concrete, which it then uses to create beautiful furniture, lighting and accessories. Its founder's goal is to produce designs that meet people's everyday needs while remaining aesthetically true to the materials used in their construction. As a spokesman for the company explains, 'We're an experimental, explorative and cross-over team … Through a series of experiments and explorations, we make each material return to its nature by revealing its original texture.' Bentu's in-house design team is driven by the belief that all materials have an inherent nobility, and that innovative design thinking has the transformative power to turn so-called lowly materials into precious treasures.

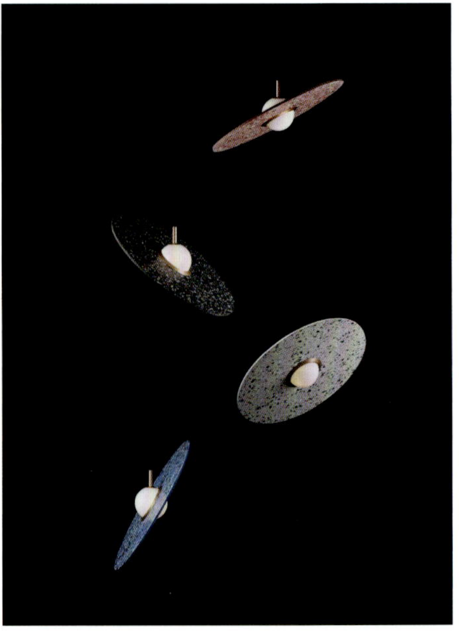

↑
PLANET PENDANT LIGHTS
by Bentu, 2018

←
H CHAIR
by Bentu, 2017

→|
I TABLES SERIES
by Bentu, 2018

BENWU STUDIO

DESIGN AS CONSTRUCTION

Benwu Studio was founded in New York City in 2013 by the designers Wang Hongchao and You Peng. Although born, raised and educated in China, both had chosen to study abroad for their masters' degrees – the former in design for luxury and craftsmanship at ECAL in Lausanne, Switzerland, and the latter in product design at the Royal College of Art in London. After completing their studies they worked as designers for various studios and companies, with Wang also undertaking a stint at Fabrica – Benetton's famous communications research centre in Treviso, Italy. In 2014 the duo designed the Bear Shelf for the PETIT H shop in Rome, which is curated by Pascale Mussard, a member of the Hermès family. This characterful yet simple construction was then customized by the PETIT H team as a 'collection piece' for Hermès. The following year three more Chinese-born designers – Ge Wei, Deng Qiyun and Geng Penglong – joined Benwu Studio as partners, each of them having a different specialization: interior architecture, product design and exhibition design respectively. This new creative blood helped Benwu Studio to become a fully fledged multidisciplinary design agency that was able to undertake all kinds of brief at its offices in Shanghai and Beijing. In terms of furniture, however, it is the team's Soft Pack sofa, which recalls the squishy nature of a Chinese steamed bun, and Sumo chair that really stand out. The latter is conceived as a demountable, flat-pack design, which is assembled without any need for glue or screws; its tenon joints simply slot into each other with the help of a few hammer taps.

↑
SOFT PACK SOFA
by Benwu Studio shown at the Cassina Showroom during the Milan Furniture Fair week, 2014 – a one-off Chinese tribute to Vico Magistretti's classic Maralunga sofa from 1973

→|
SUMO CHAIR
by Benwu Studio (self-production), 2014

ALAN CHAN

INSPIRED BY THE SILK ROAD

One of the most celebrated designers based in Hong Kong SAR, Alan Chan has won over 600 local and international awards during his illustrious career spanning five decades, which has seen him expertly balancing the roles of interior designer, brand consultant and fine artist. His Oriental Passion/Western Harmony design philosophy has not only brought him widespread international recognition, but has also been immensely influential among the younger generations of Chinese designers following in his creative wake. In 2015 his beautifully detailed and executed Silkroad seating collection was debuted at the Shanghai City Pavilion during the Milan Expo. The distinctive serpentine form of this seating range was inspired by an antique European conversation chair, which Chan has in his own private collection. This type of double-seater chair, which

Silkroad collection s chair
by Alan Chan (self-production), 2015

is also known as a tête-à-tête or lovers' seat, was primarily conceived to facilitate conversation or the sharing of ideas. This function led Chan to think too about the historic Silk Road trading route, which was crucial in the exchange of goods, services and knowledge between East and West. After meticulously studying the form and function of his antique chair, Chan came up with his own interpretation of it. This elegant S-shaped design was intended, according to him, to be all about sharing and to reflect the balance between 'East and West, Past and Present, Craftsmanship and Technology, Functionality and Form, Men and Women, Yin and Yang'. Chan's love of Chinese tea culture later inspired a matching tea ceremony table set, similarly distinguished by an East-meets-West minimalist aesthetic, and executed exquisitely in handcrafted dark walnut.

SAMUEL CHAN

ROOTED IN DESIGN ANCESTRY

Although Samuel Chan was trained in the British cabinet-making tradition, age-old Chinese typologies, forms and motifs also inspire his designs. In fact, the vast majority of his designs channel a deep-rooted Chinese spirit. That's why the name of his UK-based furniture company, Channels (which is also a pun on his surname), is so perfect in describing his Sino-influenced approach to design. His Motley floor lamps, for example, echo the form of traditional Chinese paper lanterns, while his Motley II Cedar Drum stools are modern reworkings of traditional Chinese drum stools. Chan's skilful blending of Eastern and Western design sensibilities

→
Motley floor lamps
by Samuel Chan for Channels, 2009

↓
Motley tall baton chairs
by Samuel Chan for Channels, 2010

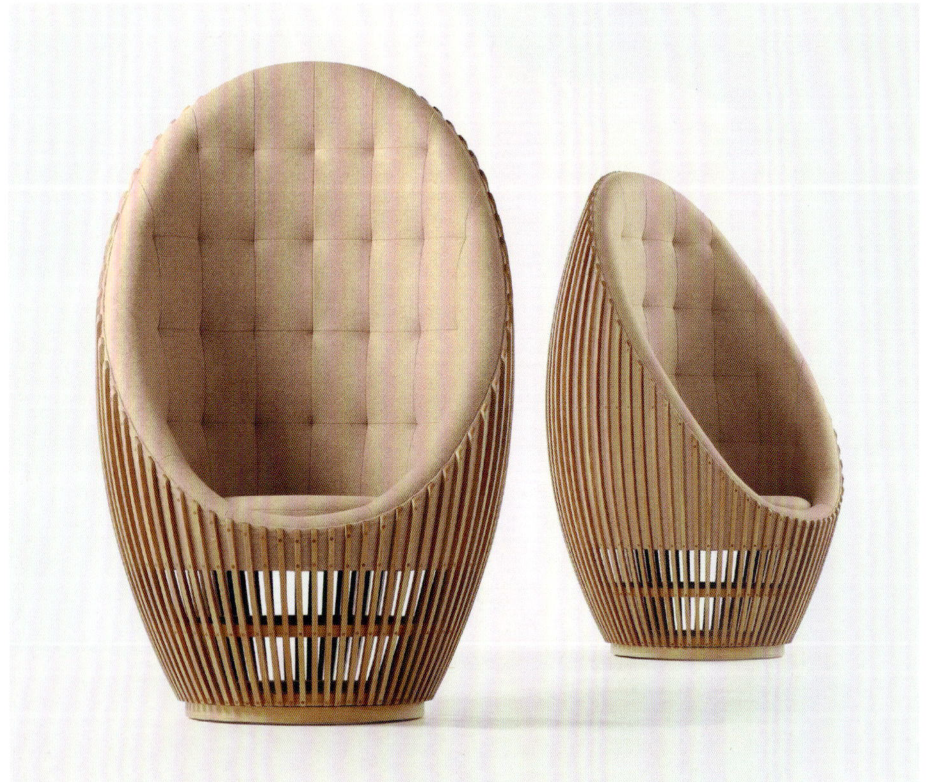

eventually led (in 2011) to a commission to create all the furniture for the landmark Jumeirah Himalayas Hotel in Shanghai. The result was a number of wonderfully evocative public spaces that fuse a nostalgic 'Memories of China' aesthetic with a sense of international contemporary hotel chic. But more than this, guided by his strong Christian faith, Chan is a deeply moral designer, who approaches all aspects of his work and life with absolute integrity. For him, the goal is 'an undivided completeness and totality', and his designs are fundamentally inspired by his sense of higher purpose, the result being that the quality of his work is truly outstanding.

→
Samuel Chan's furniture in the central foyer of the Jumeirah Himalayas Hotel in Pudong, Shanghai, 2011

CRAFT PRINCIPLES
+ DESIGN PURITY

Samuel Chan was born in Hong Kong SAR and spent his early childhood there, before emigrating to London with his family in 1979. He found the first few years at his comprehensive school in Wandsworth 'very tough', as he was barely able to understand English, yet was expected to study the works of Shakespeare and learn French. He did, however, find solace in his woodwork classes with his kindly carpentry teacher, Mr Knock, who took pity on him and gave him a 'get out of class card' in the form of a signed piece of plywood that allowed him to bunk off his English and French classes and go to the school's woodwork shop instead. It was there that he learned exacting carpentry skills, and it was Mr Knock's suggestion that he attend the London College of Furniture, before going on to study design at Middlesex University and what is now Buckinghamshire University in High Wycombe, the latter being one of the top furniture design schools in the world. After graduating Chan worked for a leading interior design consultancy, and in his free time, he continued designing and making his own pioneering New Chinese designs. Chan eventually opened his own furniture gallery, Channels, in London's New King's Road in 1995. Since then, he has won a string of awards for his East-meets-West furniture designs, which are guided by his strong belief in the ethics of craft principles and design purity – in other words, quality and simplicity.

↤
Magnus chair
by Samuel Chan for Channels, 2015

→
Column shelving units
by Samuel Chan for Channels, 2015

↓
Motley ii baton drum stools/tables
by Samuel Chan for Channels, 2008

CHEN DARUI/MAXMARKO

SINO-ELEGANCE

Chen Darui was born and raised in the city of Jiaozuo in Henan Province, which is not only the renowned birthplace of Tai Chi, but also home to the Jiaying Taoist Temple, which was built during the Qing dynasty. This spiritually laden cultural background informs Chen's predominantly Taoist outlook on life, and has helped to shape his thoughtful approach to design. When he was studying design in Beijing some 20 years ago, however, only Western design history was being taught, and the teaching was focused on, as he puts it, 'the accepted Western system'. Even back then, Chen felt that 'something was missing', so he began exploring Chinese furniture history and, as a result, came to believe that there was a real need to find common design ground between East and West. Yet, set against the context of New Chinese Design, Chen is also mindful that there is no point in slavishly re-creating the past per se, for 'today we have planes, so it is foolish to ride a horse'. Instead, through his furniture design, he seeks a Taoist balance between Eastern and Western design sensibilities, with his work referencing traditional Chinese forms but in a very pared-down European way. Chen's designs, such as the stunning Butterfly coffee table, which was inspired by the insect's figure-of-eight flight path, or his Drum stool/table (overleaf), which is a contemporary interpretation of a traditional Chinese furniture typology, are infused with an elegant Sino-sophistication. Of all the contemporary furniture being produced today in China, Chen's designs are among the most attuned to modern Western tastes, yet remain authentically Chinese in spirit.

BUTTERFLY COFFEE TABLE
by Chen Darui for Maxmarko, 2013

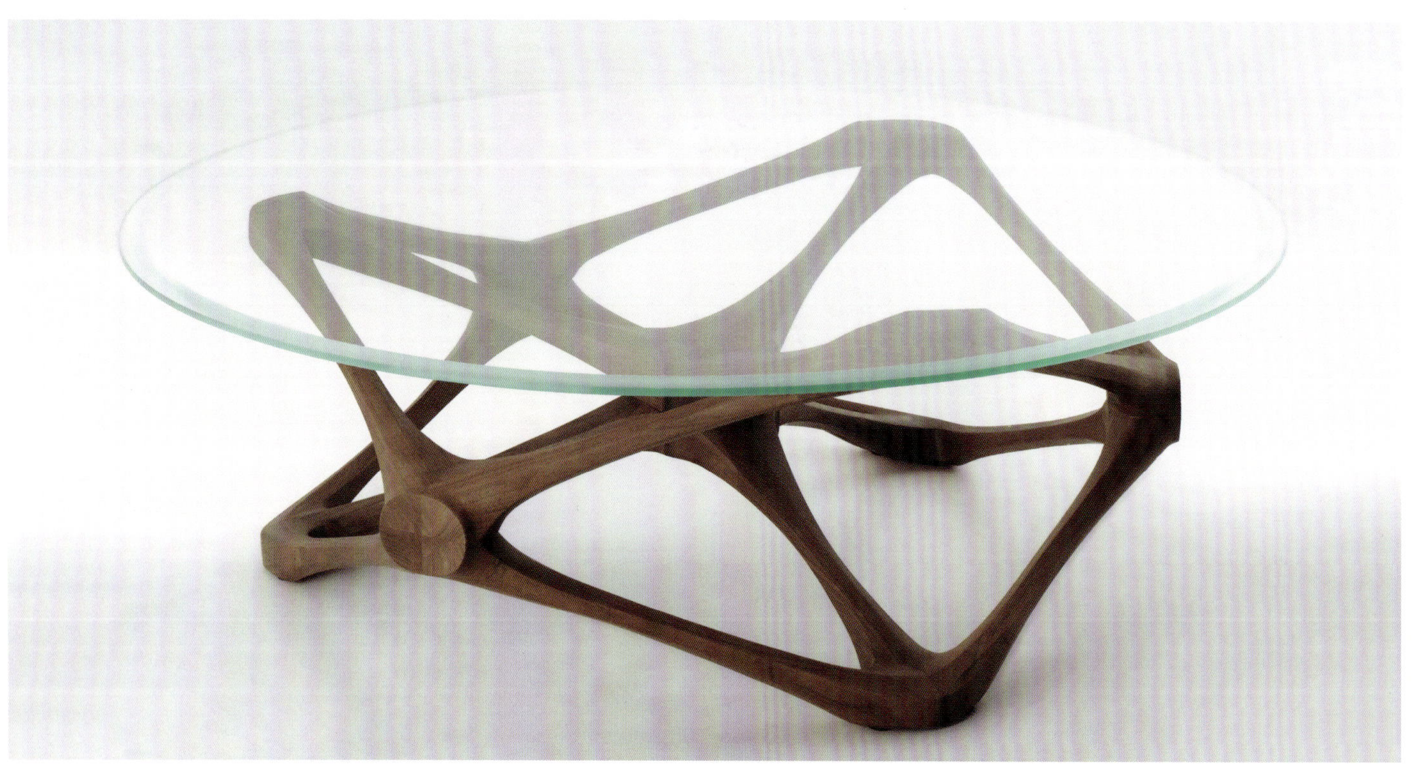

EAST MEETS WEST

After studying interior design at the Central Academy of Art and Design in Beijing, Chen Darui worked for several years as a furniture designer for various leading Chinese manufacturers, but grew tired of having to design in the 'Italian style'. In fact, his dream at this stage was to start his own brand to help forge a renaissance within Chinese furniture design. His aim was to create original designs that were a fusion of Eastern and Western influences, but back then it was not so easy to start up one's own brand. He eventually took the plunge in 2009 and established an independent design studio, founding the furniture brand Maxmarko the following year. The name is a Taoist wordplay of opposites, 'max' meaning 'large' and 'mark' signifying something as small as a dot. In fact, Chen's whole design ideology is based on the Taoist philosophy of 'harmony in diversity' and the belief that everything is created from the 'five elements'. wood, fire, earth, metal and water. Chen's mission is to achieve the Taoist goal of 'unity without uniformity', and certainly his furniture pieces, when used together in an interior, provide a distinctive signature look, while still being of interest individually thanks to his left-field design thinking. But actually, one of the most striking things about Chen's East-meets-West designs is their perfectly considered proportions and subtle combinations of materials. His beautifully executed designs are also intended to have both functional and aesthetic durability, for Chen firmly believes that enhancing the longevity of furniture is ultimately the most sustainable approach.

←
MIST SCREEN
by Chen Darui for Maxmarko, 2010

↗
CQ CHAIR
by Chen Darui for Maxmarko, 2013

→
DRUM STOOL/TABLE
by Chen Darui for Maxmarko, 2013

↓
FULL DISPLAY TEA TABLE
by Chen Darui for Maxmarko, 2017

ELEMENTAL DESIGNS

Chen Darui is not only one of China's most talented furniture designers, but also one of the most celebrated. Indeed, he became the first designer ever to be officially designated an Outstanding Cultural Figure by the government in Beijing, in 2014. His furniture designs are interesting because, although inspired by traditional Chinese forms and typologies, they are not overt in their referencing of them. In fact, it is the subtlety of Chen's designs that sets them apart. For instance, his Snow high-backed armchair obliquely references the use of screens in traditional Chinese interiors, while employing a unique construction that uses over 3,000 pieces of walnut timber cut into precise 4mm (⁵⁄₁₆in)

widths and laminated together. Likewise, his Tripod container-tables are contemporary reworkings of the traditional Ding container, which has been used for thousands of years in Chinese homes and places of worship. Similarly, the traditional lacquer boxes used to carry food in ancient Chinese palaces inspired his elegantly minimal range of Titian cabinets. Chinese characters, with the one used for 'horse' inspiring the form of his Horse rocking chair, have also influenced Chen's designs. In fact, each and every piece of Maxmarko furniture has ancient Chinese cultural roots, yet they are sensitively and skilfully expressed within a thoroughly contemporary language of design.

←
HORSE ROCKING CHAIR AND FOOTSTOOL
by Chen Darui for Maxmarko, 2011

↓
TITIAN CABINETS
by Chen Darui for Maxmarko, 2012

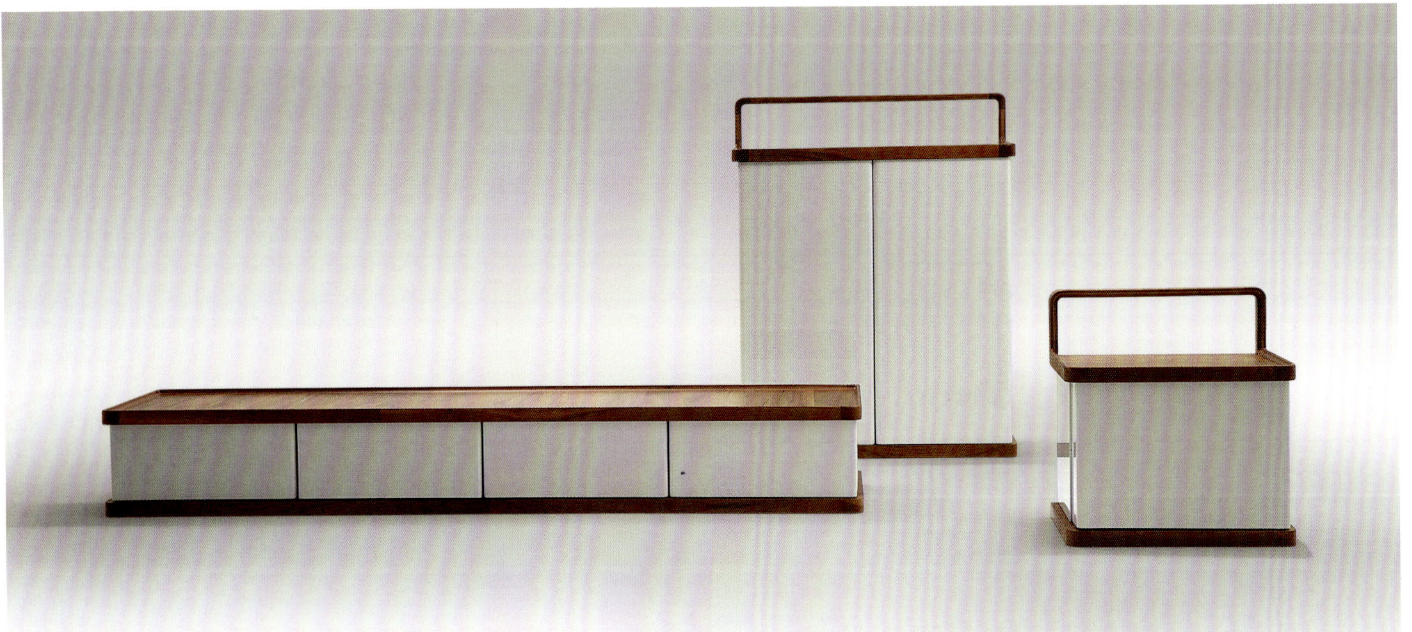

SNOW HIGH-BACKED ARMCHAIR
by Chen Darui for Maxmarko, 2010

LUNAR DINING CHAIR
by Chen Darui for Maxmarko, 2011

TRIPOD SIDE TABLE
by Chen Darui for Maxmarko, 2010

JERRY CHEN/CHUNZAI

A CONNOISSEURIAL EYE

Jerry Chen's design journey is an extremely unusual one, in that he has been able to transform his well-honed connoisseurial appreciation of Chinese art and antiques into a rare creative force that has resulted in his producing some of the most accomplished examples of New Chinese Design to date. Born in Taipei, Chen inherited his love of collecting from his mother, and as a child collected antique textiles, before moving into archaeological finds as a teenager. He initially studied ballet dancing and stage design, but abandoned these to follow his real passion: collecting antiques. He first pursued this in Hong Kong SAR, then established his own Taipei-based Chunzai cultural consultancy in 1992. Over the next three decades he became one of the most renowned dealers and collectors of historic Chinese artefacts, but also branched out into contemporary Chinese art, and curated a number of important Asian art exhibitions. During this time he amassed a truly world-class collection of period objects that had originally been designed for use within the intellectually rarefied walls of scholars' studies. As he notes, 'Collecting fuels the desire to learn, enriching life. Over and above that, collecting inspires cultivation and rumination.' But what it also does is help the collector to acquire an exacting 'eye', which can then be applied to the design of contemporary objects. And that is exactly what Chen has done through a remarkable series of furniture designs, which have been painstakingly handmade in his workshop in Xianyou by skilled craftsmen using age-old joinery techniques. Inspired by the elegant sweeping lines of calligraphy, Chen's seating designs from his Zan Zhi – In Praise of Rectitude series are intended to convey the fluidity and transparency of space and time, while rekindling the ancient Chinese scholarly spirit and formal aesthetics of Ming-style furniture. As Chen explains, 'I'm not interested in functional furniture per se; like sculpture, the proportions of a design need to be perfect. My furniture designs are about feelings, like aesthetic scholar furniture from the past; they are reflections of a state of mind … One needs to understand that China is a very spiritual culture, and we believe that objects can have a spirit.' Indeed, Chen's own designs could certainly be described as sublime distillations of pure Chinese spirit.

from Zan Zhi – In Praise of Rectitude series by Jerry Chen for Chunzai, 2010

CHAIR, WORK NO.12
from Zan Zhi – In Praise of Rectitude
series by Jerry Chen for Chunzai,
2008

→

Detail of Chair, work no.26 from Zan
Zhi – In Praise of Rectitude series by
Jerry Chen for Chunzai, 2012

EXPRESSIVE LINES

The renowned Chinese collector and designer Jerry Chen established his own furniture brand, Chunzai, in 2004, having already run a cultural agency of the same name for over a decade. His resulting furniture designs can be seen as exquisitely rendered contemporary explorations of the literati aesthetic and spirit. His scrolling chaise and chair from his Green Vine series (2012), for example, are not concerned with strict adherence to formal design rules, but instead are intended to 'channel a raw vitality and symbolize the unexpected and uncontrollable twists and turns of real life'. In fact, the inspiration for this series comes from Xu Wei, a Ming-dynasty painter and poet famed for his artistic expressiveness, who famously wrote a poem that summed up his unbridled spirit thus: 'After half a life, I am already an old man. I stand alone in my studio braving the night winds. Having no place to sell the pearls under my brush, I carelessly throw them into the wild wisteria.' Chen's choice of rattan in his designs is intended to evoke the vines of wisteria mentioned in Xu Wei's poem, and symbolize how the chaotic vitality of nature can be harnessed to make something ordered and beautiful. As he explains, 'The shaping of material from the disorder of nature into the order of human life may appear to be a kind of taming, but in fact it is an elevation into humanism through design.' In accordance with Chinese furniture-making traditions, these designs employ rosewood in their construction, but Chen completely understands what a thorny issue that is in terms of sustainability. He believes the only way to address the problem is to allow 'only the best masters to use the best wood, because otherwise it is wasted for ever'. Certainly, Chen's own designs are unequivocally masterful, a form of furniture as philosophy, which capture the essence of Chinese design both past and present.

↑
Detail of Chaise Longue, another version of Work No.9 from the Green Vine Series by Jerry Chen for Chunzai, 2013 – with a seat of 'randomly' woven rattan

←
Room installation by Jerry Chen for Chunzai, 2018 – showing a typical tea ceremony furniture arrangement

CHAIR, WORK NO.5
from Green Vine series
by Jerry Chen for Chunzai, 2012

CHAISE LONGUE, WORK NO.9
from Green Vine series
by Jerry Chen for Chunzai, 2013 –
can also be turned on its side to
become a Song-style low screen

CHEN MIN

KNOCK-DOWN FURNITURE

Born into an artistic family, Chen Min was taught Chinese calligraphy and traditional painting techniques as a very young child. His grandfather Zongzao Zhao was one of China's most famous printmakers and a professor at the prestigious China Academy of Art in Hangzhou. Not surprisingly, Chen chose to follow in his family's creative footsteps, initially studying design at the Köln International School of Design (KISD) and then at the famous Design Academy Eindhoven. He subsequently took a master's degree in industrial design at the Domus Academy in Milan, graduating in 2009. He returned to China the following year, and in 2012 established his own multidisciplinary design studio, Chen Min Office, in Hangzhou. Since then he has designed a number of innovative Neo-Chinese furniture pieces that reference traditional objects and forms, such as his knock-down Steamer series made of three modular bamboo elements that were inspired by the form and construction of traditional dumpling steamers. Likewise, Min's Chair uses modern production technology to explore the construction of Ming furniture in a modern and innovative way based on demountable elements, while his Y–table is also based on a system of elements that can be connected to make up not only a trestle-like design, but also a bench and a bed.

↑
GONG SHELVING SYSTEM
by Chen Min (self-production), 2012

→
GONG TABLE
by Chen Min (self-production), 2012

MU COAT RACK
by Chen Min (self-production), 2013 – also
known as the Jungle coat rack, here it is shown
with an early prototypical model

CHARACTERFUL ELEMENTALISM

Many of Chen Min's furniture designs are distinguished by a strong elemental quality. For example, his Mu coat rack, also known as the Jungle, was initially conceived at prototype stage as three stacked elements that take the form of the Chinese character *mu*, meaning 'tree'. In Chinese writing, when three *mu* are combined they become the character for *sen*, meaning 'jungle', so in effect this design is a play on words that refers to the origin of the material it is made of. The design's final form, with its 12 branching elements, certainly expresses the formal essence of a tree, while also providing a practical and stable, simple yet useful piece of furniture. Similarly, Chen Min has played with the design potential of another Chinese character known as *gong*, the origins of which derive from a very distinctive structural element found in the roof trusses of ancient Chinese buildings. This component is made of two T-shaped forms inverted and set at 90 degrees to each other. Chen has combined this repeating element to create not only a simple yet stylish minimalist table, but also a colourful modular shelving system with infinite constructional possibilities.

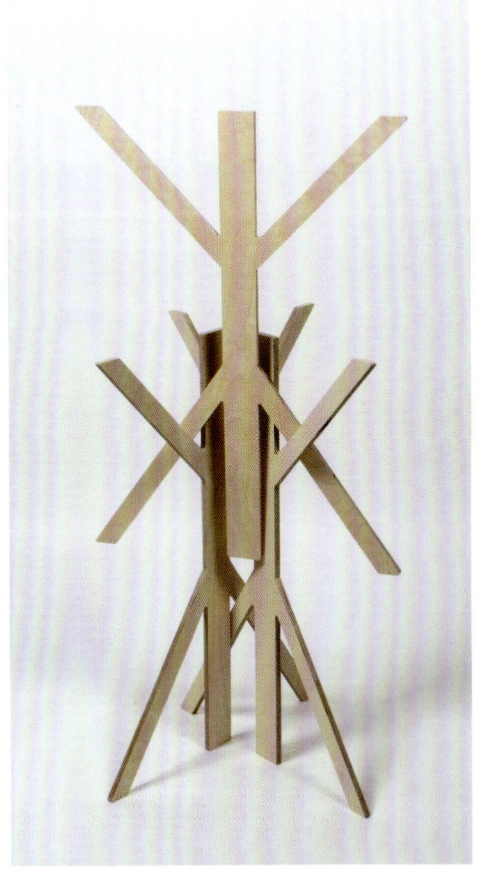

CHEN MIN + SCOTT LIN

CALLIGRAPHIC INFLUENCES +
LOOPING FORMS

The Bow-tie chair and the Hangzhou stool are well-known contemporary Chinese seating designs that reflect the stylistic influence of the elegant looping forms found in Chinese calligraphy. The former, by Scott Lin, is constructed from 13 strips of heat-bent bamboo, making it lightweight yet with an inherent springy resilience and airy ventilation. The three 'holes' that are incorporated into the chair's looping form can also be used for storage, although this would certainly detract from the design's wonderful gestural lines. Chen Min's arc-shaped stool likewise has a strong visual presence, in this case because of its innovative sprung form, which is made of 16 sheets of bamboo veneer, each only 0.9mm (1/16 in) thick, which are held under tension using a simple bamboo strut. The design's name refers to Chen Min's birthplace, the ancient cultural centre of Hangzhou in Zhejiang province. The sections of his stool fan out like the rippling waters of the West Lake, the city's most famous scenic attraction. A finalist in the Loewe Foundation Craft Prize in 2018, the Hangzhou stool is noteworthy for its combination of aesthetic refinement and technical accomplishment.

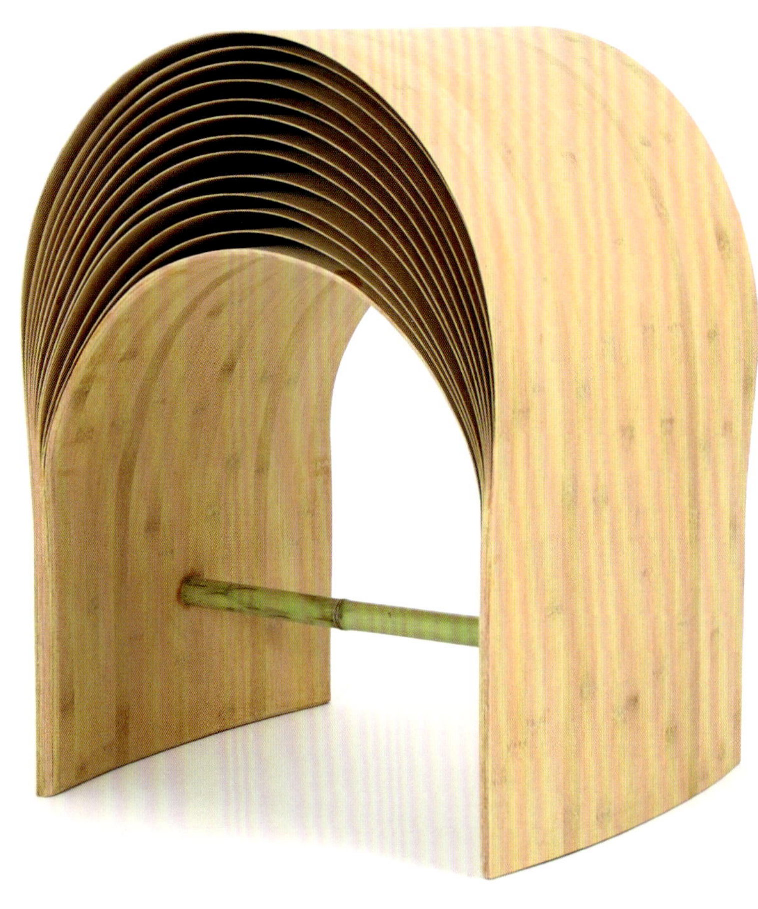

Hangzhou stool
by Chen Min (self-production), 2013

BOW-TIE CHAIR
by Scott Lin for Gridesign, 2015

CHINESE RED + SPATIAL GEOMETRY

A recognized pioneer of modern interior design in China, Chen Xiangjing originally studied at Beijing's Central Academy of Fine Arts, graduating in 1982, and subsequently taught at the Guangzhou Academy of Fine Arts. In 1989 he moved to the United Kingdom in order to continue his studies at Manchester Metropolitan University. On returning to China in 1992, he helped to establish the interior design and construction firm Guangzhou Newsdays, and worked as its chief designer. In this role he was responsible for various award-winning schemes, which led to his being named one of Asia's top ten designers in 2007. After 30 years in the interior design business, Chen decided in 2015 to set up his own design research office, Jing Design. Around the same time, he also established his own furniture manufacturing company to produce his eye-catching line of Neo-Ming furniture, which incorporates 'Chinese Red' hand-lacquering. As Chen explains, 'for me, red symbolizes nostalgia and reunion. But lacquer does not only have symbolic value; it is a craft process with very ancient roots in China, and it is also sustainable and helps to conserve wood.' By contrast, his Yi series, made of oak or ash, has a younger and less historicizing look, yet its strict spatial geometry is still pure Chinese in spirit. With its formal restraint and unadorned surfaces, this range successfully channels the ancient literati aesthetic in a thoroughly contemporary way.

←
<u>MING SERIES HIGH-BACKED ARMCHAIR</u>
by Chen Xiangjing for Jing Living, 2016 – a modern interpretation of an historic model known as the 'Official's Hat' chair because the form of its crest rail echoes that of the headgear worn by scholar-officials in the Song dynasty

↑↑
<u>YI SERIES TABLE</u>
by Chen Xiangjing for Jing Living, 2018

↑
<u>YI SERIES SIDE TABLE</u>
by Chen Xiangjing for Jing Living, 2018

CALLIGRAPHIC FURNITURE

Chen Yanfei's first artistic love was calligraphy, which he learned as a child, and certainly the controlled yet characterful lines of his furniture designs reflect his well-honed ink and brush skills. Like a number of other enlightened furniture designers of his generation, Chen looks back to look forward in order to create contemporary designs that are authentically Chinese, with a strongly rooted cultural identity. But more than this, his furniture pieces convey an atmosphere of poetic and scholarly thoughtfulness traditionally associated with the practice of calligraphy. Some of his designs are also created specifically for spiritual contemplation, hence their straight backs and wide seats, which enable sitters (if they wish) to assume a cross-legged meditation pose. Chen believes that designers should not be too narrow in their interpretation of historic Chinese furniture forms, but rather should innovate refined modern evolutions of them in order to produce designs that fit with today's lifestyles while still possessing a strong cultural resonance.

↑↑
HARMONY CHAIR
by Chen Yanfei for Pusu, 2015

↑
YAZHI LARGE MEDITATION COUCH BED
by Chen Yanfei for Pusu, 2012

←
YONGMEI DINING TABLE
by Chen Yanfei for Pusu, 2013

→
PUMPKIN STOOL
by Chen Yanfei for Pusu, 2012 – shown alongside a calligraphic work of art by Chen

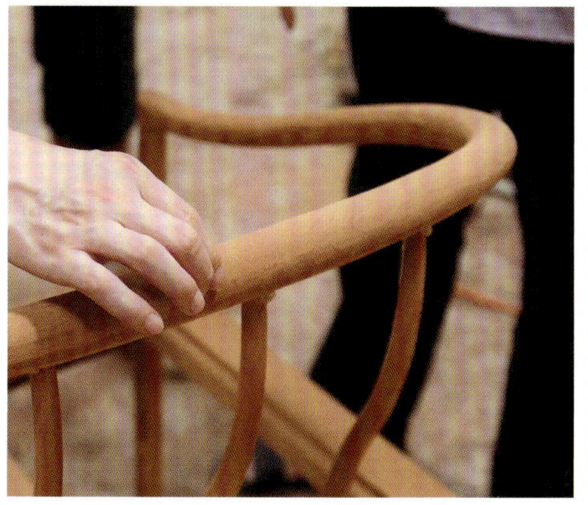

↑
Views of Pusu's furniture workshop, showing the making of the Tiandi Horseshoe chair

↓
TIANDI HORSESHOE ARMCHAIR
by Chen Yanfei for Pusu, 2012

A CHAIR IN THE MAKING

Chen Yanfei's company Pusu is well-known in Asian design circles for the exemplary quality of its furniture, which is noted as much for its exquisite craftsmanship as for its beautifully simplified Neo-Ming forms. Employing traditional Chinese cabinet-making techniques along with age-old craft skills, such as bamboo weaving, Chen's furniture, with its stripped-down essentialism, exemplifies the very best attributes of the New Chinese design movement. The perfect proportions and subtle lines of his Tiandi Horseshoe armchair, for example, are in total harmony with the human body, while its unadorned elegance gives it a rare timeless quality that transcends fashion. This is a design for contemporary aesthetes, the spiritual descendants of Chinese scholars, who can appreciate that simplicity in design, when handled deftly, is often the highest expression of refinement. Such pieces also reflect the proud cultural specificity of what is sometimes called *huaren* design, meaning design specifically created within and ultimately for Chinese-speaking communities.

FROM LEFT TO RIGHT:
Tiandi yokeback chair, Qingyuan clothes rack,
Tiandi table (with 'Giant's Arm Braces'), Tiandi
Horseshoe chair, Pumpkin stool, Tiandi couch,
tray/table and Tiandi stool – all by Chen Yanfei
for Pusu

PLAIN AND SIMPLE

In the vanguard of New Chinese design, the Pusu company is well known for producing furniture representative of the contemporary *huaren* style and with a rare aesthetic refinement. The venture's founder, Chen Yanfei, comes from a family of medical practitioners who encouraged their younger generation to take up hobbies. Consequently, and unusually among his contemporaries, Chen studied calligraphy from a very young age. This led him to train as a graphic designer at the Guangzhou Academy of Fine Arts, and on graduation he worked as a designer for various magazines. It was during this period that Chen's interest in furniture was sparked, and he began thinking about how he could combine his love of calligraphy with this newfound passion. In 2006 he designed his first piece of furniture, which was executed by a master craftsman in Xitang specially for Chen's newly acquired home in Guangzhou. The following year he got a job with the high-end *Home Gallery* interiors magazine, which gave him the confidence and knowledge to establish his own Guangzhou-based furniture brand, Pusu, in 2011. Meaning 'simple and plain', the company's name was inspired by a quotation from the poet Chuang Tzu: 'When something is simple and plain, none under the heavens can rival it in beauty.'

CHEN YOU-DE + LIN CHIN-HUA

A CHINESE PUZZLE

Chen You-De and Lin Chin-Hua's Burr Puzzle high stool is a stunning experimental design that seems at first glance to be a chaotic mess of barely contained aluminium wires. With its playful scribble-like composition, it is as though someone's random doodle has been magically lifted off a page and given three-dimensional reality. Yet it is actually a much more considered design than it might initially appear, for its construction relies on the clever adaptation of traditional mortise and tenon joints, which have been used in Chinese furniture-making for over 5,000 years. Chen You-De and Lin Chin-Hua, however, chose to replace wood with colour-anodized aluminium wires to achieve the stabilizing mortise joints that allow their dynamic high stool not only to stand, but also to support the weight of a person. The whole concept behind this unusual seating design was inspired by Chinese burr puzzles, hence its name. As with these puzzles, which comprise interlocking notched sticks that can be combined to create a 'puzzle knot', the Burr Puzzle high stool is assembled by placing its elements in a very specific sequence so that they lock together to form a firm and solid structure.

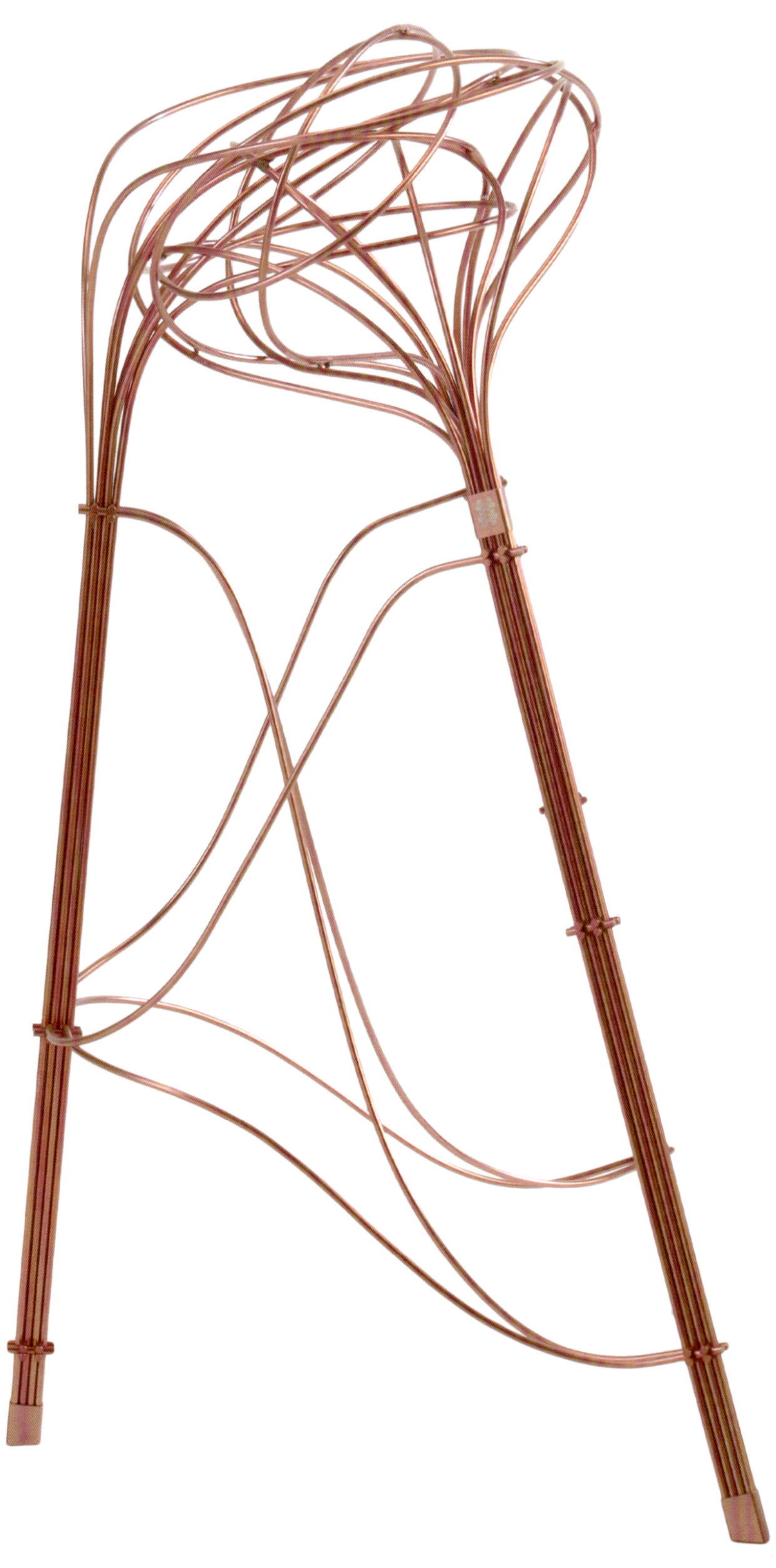

→

Burr puzzle high stool
by Chen You-De and Lin Chin-Hua
for Gallery ALL, 2013

→|

Detail of the Burr Puzzle high stool,
showing its stabilizing mortise
and tenon joints

ADRIAN CHENG + SHIGERU UCHIDA

AN ARTISANAL
DESIGN ADVENTURE

The real-estate magnate and jewellery empire scion Adrian Cheng, who's based in Hong Kong SAR, is on a mission 'to create a contemporary Chinese culture'. His K11 Art Foundation, established in 2010, is a high-profile, not-for-profit organization that over the last decade has promoted and supported emerging Chinese artists by showcasing their work in local, regional and international exhibitions. In 2014 *ArtReview*'s Power 100 List named Cheng as one of the most influential figures in the art world. Three years later he collaborated with the renowned Japanese designer Shigeru Uchida on the design of a new furniture collection called Khora, which was first showcased at the 'Wander from Within' exhibition during the Salone del Mobile in Milan. As Cheng noted at the exhibition, 'Furniture is often associated

Detail of <u>AU1 CHAIR</u>

↗
<u>AU2 TABLE</u>
from Khora collection
by Adrian Cheng and Shigeru Uchida
(self-production), 2016–17

→
<u>AU1 CHAIR</u>
from Khora collection
by Adrian Cheng and Shigeru Uchida
(self-production), 2016–17

⇥
<u>AU3 CHAIR</u>
from Khora collection
by Adrian Cheng and Shigeru Uchida
(self-production), 2016–17

with home, enclosures and comfort with specific roles to play. What if furniture is designed to go beyond the boundary of physical sensibility, to sever one's physical connection from daily life, channelling the mind to live in the ephemeral, singular moment far from the ordinary?' With this aim, the Khora collection, which was inspired by Japanese landscapes and tea ceremonies, cleverly bridges the gap between art furniture and artisanal craft, and comprises seats and tables wrapped in woven or gridded screens that cast interesting and evocative shadow patterns. The pieces are handmade by Japanese craftsmen and executed in chestnut and bamboo, while also featuring traditional *washi* (mulberry bark) paper and lacquering techniques in their construction. While this remarkably poetic furniture collection was Cheng's first foray into furniture design, it was Uchida's last, as he died in 2016. Nonetheless, Cheng says, 'There will definitely be more furniture in the future.'

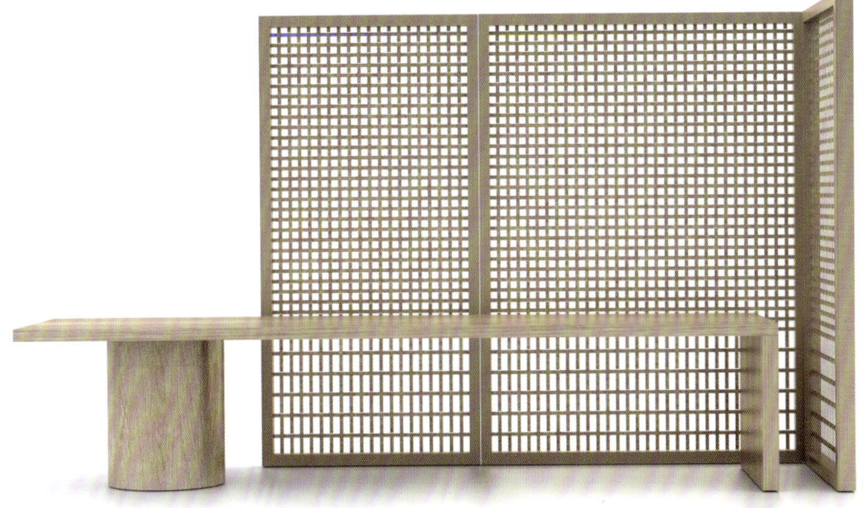

FRANK CHOU

CHINESE MINIMALISM

A rising star of contemporary Chinese design, Frank Chou is a highly talented innovator who is on a personal mission to reform design and manufacture in China. Interestingly, he studied material science and engineering at Beijing Forestry University and received no formal training as a designer. His natural design talents, however, are self-evident in his already impressive body of work. This unusual academic pathway explains his interest in creating sustainable designs, as well as his ability to deftly handle the manufacturing side of design. Initially, he tried to convince well-established Chinese manufacturers to produce his designs, but he found they were too entrenched in their old ways of doing things and unreceptive to aesthetic change. All too often he heard the worn-out excuse that 'modern design costs too much' or was 'too risky' commercially. Frustrated, Chou eventually started his own design-led brand, and the sleek New Chinese designs he began self-producing helped to build his reputation as one to watch among both his design peers and consumers. Today, he not only manufactures his own designs, but also works as a designer for a number of other forward-looking furniture brands, creating pieces that intelligently balance practical function with refined aesthetic purity.

MODERN ORIENTALISM

Utterly committed to promoting responsible design, Frank Chou tries whenever possible to communicate the goals of good design through design forums, cultural exchanges and exhibitions. He believes that in China there is still a big need for, as he puts it, 'industrial upgrading' and 'design education popularization', because the more informed that manufacturers and consumers become about the ethical goals of good design, the better choices they will make in terms of sustainability. Indeed, when it comes to his own designs, he is very conscious of the environmental impact of the materials and processes he employs, and therefore tries to create designs that have an inherent physical durability as well as aesthetic longevity. He also mindfully designs furniture that is culturally relevant in order to establish all-important emotional connections. He does this by referencing archetypal Chinese forms in thoroughly innovative and contemporary ways. His bold, reductivist strain of modern orientalism is actually very distinctive, and gives his furniture pieces, such as his highly regarded Kong Chair, Stack table and Rong desk, an undeniable 'signature' character born of sculptural confidence.

↑↑
RONG DESK
by Frank Chou for Zizaoshe, 2016

↑
KONG CHAIR
by Frank Chou (self-production), 2016

↑
STACK TABLE
by Frank Chou (self-production), 2018

→
<u>Suson coffee table</u>
by Frank Chou for Roling Liang Chen, 2017

↓
<u>Cube armchair</u>
by Frank Chou for FNJI, 2018

↘
<u>Combo sofa</u>
by Frank Chou (self-production), 2018

ELEMENTAL FORMS

Frank Chou's designs are often characterized by geometric abstraction and functional playfulness. His self-produced Combo sofa, for instance, is an attempt to reinvent the 'classic' sofa by splicing it into six modular units covered in different materials associated with traditional upholstery, namely leather, woollen textile and cloth. The asymmetry of this design is refreshingly original, yet it has been accomplished with the minimum of means. His Cube armchair is similarly constructed, using blocks of upholstery that are asymmetrically composed, giving it a quirky visual interest as well as a characterful presence. Chou's interest in abstracted elemental forms can also be seen in his table designs for Roling Liang Chen, with the hexagonal Lonan side tables inspired by both oriental aesthetics and philosophy. While the lacquered surfaces of these designs are meant to enhance an Asian sense of lightness and rich colour, their coalescence of flat and curved planes also intentionally references the Eastern belief that combining opposites can create harmony. Similarly, his Suson coffee table unites round and square forms in a balanced composition, and, as Chou notes, its forest of criss-crossed legs supporting the disc-like marble top give the design 'a sense of natural philosophy'.

LONAN SIDE TABLES
by Frank Chou for Roling Liang Chen, 2017

THE CHINESE FAN

Before establishing his own design studio, Frank Chou worked in Europe for a while, an experience that gave him a rare and expansive understanding of the furniture industry. He has a good grasp not only of how to design furniture, but also how to manufacture and market it. As a result, when people ask, 'Who will become the Chinese Tom Dixon?', the odds are that it will be Chou. One of his greatest strengths as a designer is that he has a definable signature style that comes from his being constantly inspired by Chinese cultural references, which he skilfully appropriates to create innovative and daring furniture designs that have a globally appealing East-meets-West aesthetic. His Fan series of chairs and flat-pack tables is an excellent example of this, with the forms of the tabletops and chair backs being inspired by the simple stick-and-circle construction of traditional rigid Chinese fans. However, as Chou notes, 'We don't want to follow traditional Chinese styles, but at the same time we need to figure out what makes Modern Chinese different to Western styles. The challenge is to find our own design language.' And that is exactly what he and his team are doing with a gusto and determination that are pure Frank Chou.

←
Fan side table
by Frank Chou (self-production), 2016

→|
Various models from the fan chair series
by Frank Chou (self-production), 2017

HAMUOO

FURNITURE FOR SMALL PEOPLE

The concept of family is the bedrock of Chinese society. Owing to the one-child policy, which has only recently been relaxed, young children tend to be exceptionally doted on by their parents and grandparents. In terms of furniture design and production, this means that practically every Chinese design-led furniture brand, from 8 Hours and Lost&Found to Maxmarko and Thrudesign, has innovative pieces in its product line specifically intended for children. Often these pieces have come about because the designers initially created them for their own children, and only subsequently put them into production. This focus on child-centred design has also inspired the founding of a few dedicated children's furniture brands, of which Hamuoo is one of the most interesting and high-profile. Adhering to principles of 'refinement and simplicity', Hamuoo creates child-size furniture of refreshing originality and playfulness. Especially noteworthy is its range of

diminutive chairs, which take the form of different Chinese zodiac animals, including Mini Monkey, Clever Rat, Diligent Ox, Brave Tiger, Astute Rabbit, Flying Dragon and Agile Snake. Hamuoo uses a combination of hardwoods accredited by the Forest Stewardship Council (FSC) – namely, North American black walnut, American hard maple and American red cherry – and ingeniously contrasts the colours of these woods to create its characterful pieces, which are constructed using traditional Chinese mortise and tenon joints. Exemplifying contemporary Chinese woodcraft at its best, Hamuoo's designs have an endearing innocence that invites imaginative creative play.

↑
PARTNER BEDSIDE CABINET
by Yang Xuguang for Hamuoo, 2018

←
ASTUTE RABBIT CHAIR
by Yang Xuguang for Hamuoo, 2017

↙
MINI MONKEY CHAIR
by Yang Xuguang for Hamuoo, 2016

↓
DILIGENT OX CHAIR
by Yang Xuguang for Hamuoo, 2017

→|
Child sitting on a Diligent Ox chair

TAOIST-INSPIRED DESIGN

For Hong Wei, the term 'oriental' implies concepts that dwell in the metaphysical realm, which can be embodied in material objects. In Taoist philosophy, it is believed that objects are imbued with spirits and that all human activity should be in accord with nature. As Hong notes, 'What I care about most is how it feels to be human … Design is about relationships … The highest state of being that design can reach is through the delivery of concepts.' This attitude is not so surprising once you learn that Hong is by training and profession a skilled visual communicator, who over the last decade or so has been an influential advocate of infusing graphic design with relevant Chinese content. He is now doing this same thing within the realm of furniture design with spectacular results. The three Ming-inspired designs shown here alongside one of his beautiful artworks reveal an almost spiritual distillation of form, as well as exemplary Zen-like craftsmanship. Hong's goal is to provoke a Zen state of human experience by creating furniture that is infused with oriental philosophy and that unifies the wisdom of traditional craftsmanship with an elegant simplicity suited to contemporary lifestyles.

↑
Calligraphic poster
by Hong Wei featuring
his Pin Yi chair, 2017

↑
Pin Yi chair
by Hong Wei for Wei, 2016

→
Jian chair
by Hong Wei for Wei, 2014

GUI CHAIR
by Hong Wei for Wei, 2016

CENG CHAIR
by Hong Wei for Wei, 2016

MING INFLUENCES

Although Hong Wei's furniture is inspired by historic Chinese archetypes, symbolic forms, decorative motifs and age-old methods of construction, he is able to distil the very essence of their Chinese-ness into highly abstracted forms that have a potent sculptural modernity. Describing this *huaren* design spirit as 'oriental rhyme', Hong is mindful that Chinese design should not, as he puts it, 'fall into the narrow cracks of nationalism' nor go 'in the direction of contemporary Western modernism', because that would lead to 'a titanic fiasco, a flop'. Instead, using traditional Chinese *sun mao* (mortise and tenon) joinery techniques, Hong creates Neo-Ming pieces that are perfectly proportioned, three-dimensional summations of age-old Chinese forms, yet translated into a thoroughly contemporary language of design. Encapsulating the spirit of oriental philosophy, Hong's exquisitely designed and executed chairs are supreme examples of modern *huaren* design at its masterful best.

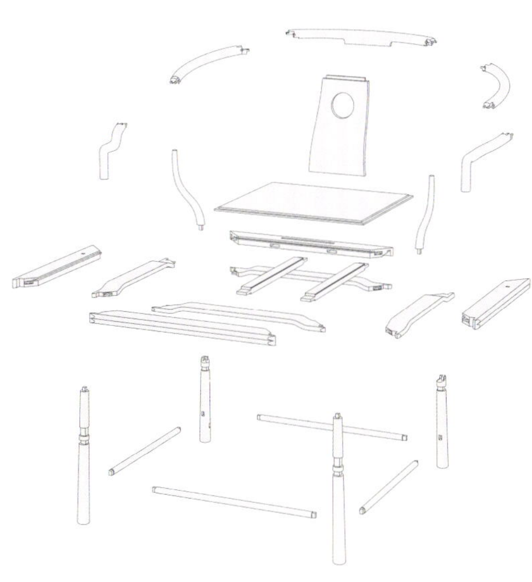

↑
Constructional diagram
of the Ceng chair

↗↗
CLOUD CHAIR
by Hong Wei for Wei, 2018

↗
KUAN CHAIR
by Hong Wei for Wei, 2016

→
WEN CHAIR
by Hong Wei for Wei, 2018

THE PUZZLING CHAIR

Hong Wei is a multi-award-winning graphic designer and creative director, who is a member of the prestigious AGI (Alliance Graphique Internationale). Well known in his field, he also designs furniture, thereby – unusually – spanning the worlds of 2D and 3D design. His Neo-Ming furniture designs are notable for their powerful elemental quality and bold graphic outlines. In fact, one test of a truly iconic design is whether it can be identified solely from its silhouette, and Hong Wei's designs easily achieve that because the profiles of his furniture pieces have such graphic strength. Of all his designs, however, the most technically accomplished and aesthetically impressive is his remarkable Xi armchair, which was inspired by traditional Chinese burr puzzles. These are made from notched pieces of wood that lock together sequentially and resemble the prickly seed cases called burrs. The Xi chair's complex 327-piece construction is not only a masterful demonstration of Chinese ingenuity and craftsmanship, but also possesses a compelling sculptural quality that is all about the play of light and shadow, solid and void, yin and yang.

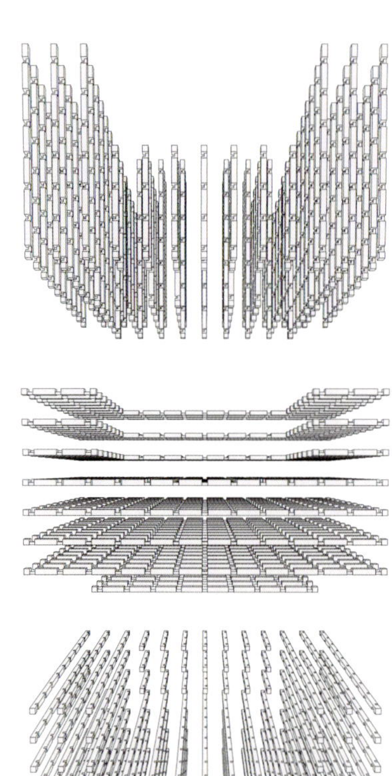

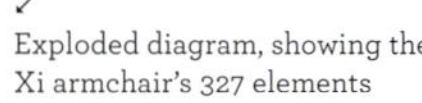

Exploded diagram, showing the Xi armchair's 327 elements

XI ARMCHAIR
by Hong Wei for Wei, 2016

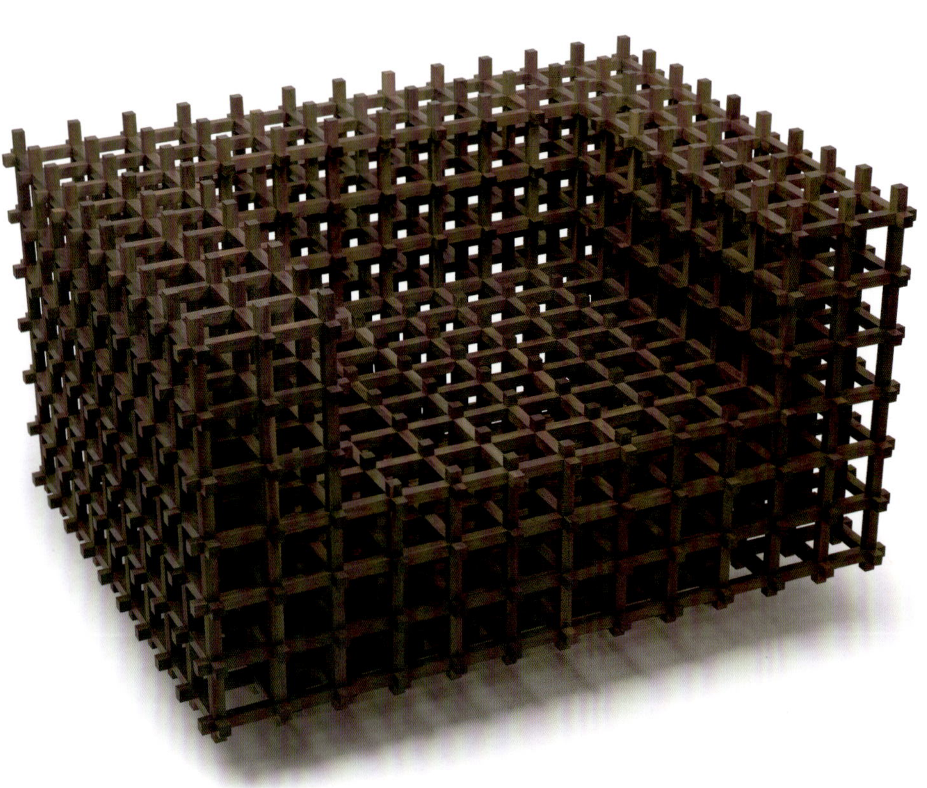

Detail of the Xi armchair,
showing its puzzle-like construction

HOU ZHENG-GUANG/MORELESS

DESIGNS FOR TEA

Unless you are Chinese, or lucky enough to have been given an insider's tour of China, it is quite difficult to understand the importance of tea culture in Chinese society. In fact, taking tea plays a central role in facilitating social interaction of all kinds, and, as a result, a formal ritual has grown up around it. Given this, it is not surprising that most Chinese furniture manufacturers produce tea-table sets – indeed, they come in all shapes and sizes, and at prices for every pocket. Hou Zheng-Guang's Three Walkers tea table and matching stools set is, however, one of the most successful products of its type in terms of innovative compact design. This small yet highly sculptural furniture group was inspired by a Confucian observation: 'If I am walking with two other people, at least one of them can be my teacher.' The spiralling forms of the group's pieces have a strong dynamic presence, which helps to accentuate the undeniable beauty of their laminated walnut block construction. Equally beautiful and visually dynamic is Hou's Big Fish tea table with its matching stools and bench. The asymmetrical shape of the table suggests the sweeping form of a large fish underwater. Possessing a refined yet engaging organic quality, both these suites of tea furniture have a calm yet modern Zen-like aesthetic, utterly perfect for their intended ritualized function.

↑

THREE WALKERS TEA TABLE AND STOOLS
by Hou Zheng-Guang for MoreLess, 2006

↓ & →
BIG FISH TEA TABLE, BENCH AND STOOLS
by Hou Zheng-Guang for MoreLess, 2015

Born in 1972, Hou Zheng-Guang initially studied design in China before taking a master's degree in furniture design at Buckinghamshire New University in High Wycombe. Often just called 'High Wycombe', this college is regarded as one of the world's premier teaching colleges for furniture design – indeed, the famous British designers Robin Day and Lucian Ercolani are among its alumni. Importantly, the college has always maintained strong links to the local furniture industry, which means that its students tend to have a good hands-on understanding of manufacturing. Certainly, Hou learned his lessons well there, and on returning to China started his own successful design career. In 2009 he stepped up to the challenge of founding his own furniture and lifestyle brand, MoreLess, and within just three years he had become widely recognized as one of China's most influential designers. His success comes down to his ability to create furniture that is a delicate fusion of Eastern and Western cultural influences. Applying a European predilection for simplicity to evolved historic Chinese forms, Hou's work is exemplified by practical function and aesthetic beauty, the latter being an outcome of the former. Employing natural materials, simplified forms and high-quality craftsmanship, Hou's designs also accentuate the exquisiteness of their detailing. But more than this, his understated work always falls within the realm of what is universally understood as good design, which makes his MoreLess stores veritable emporiums of good taste.

↑
TREASURE CABINET
by Hou Zheng-Guang for MoreLess, 2009

6 DIMENSIONS MODULAR COFFEE TABLE
by Hou Zheng-Guang for MoreLess, 2018

→
SU ZHOU MODULAR STORAGE UNITS
by Hou Zheng-Guang for MoreLess, 2006

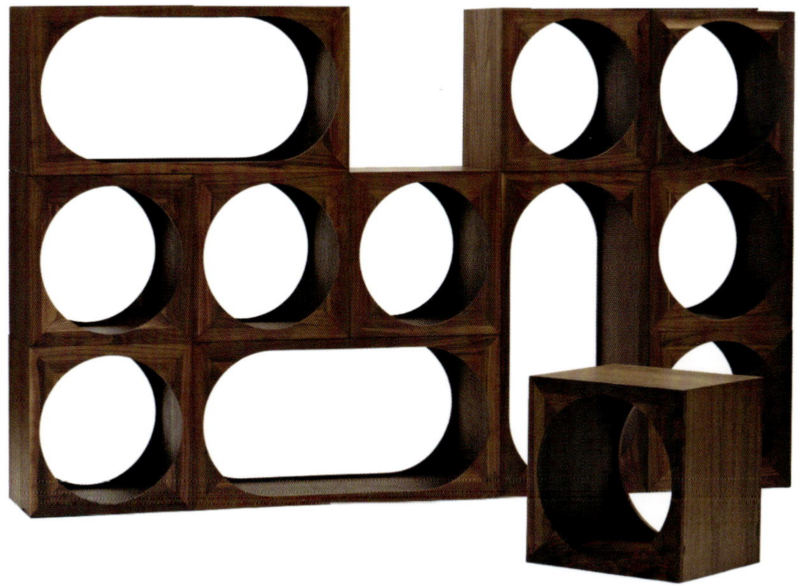

MEMORIES OF MING

In many ways the New Chinese School has parallels with the Arts and Crafts movement in Britain during the late nineteenth and early twentieth centuries, in that it seeks to revive indigenous craft traditions and historic ideal furniture forms in order to create work that is contemporary yet also retains a connection to the past. Hou Zheng-Guang's refined designs, which are essentially distillations of ideal Ming forms, exemplify this new Chinese Arts and Crafts approach probably better than any other designer's work. This is not surprising, given that he undertook his design training in High Wycombe, the heartland of Britain's furniture industry. The aesthetic refinement, thoughtful functionality and beautiful craftsmanship of Hou's designs as well as those by other designers associated with MoreLess, as evinced in the warm-hued walnut shelves, chairs and stool shown here, not only set the brand apart from many of its competitors, but also will no doubt ensure that its furniture will become the much-loved antiques of tomorrow.

You jie chair
by Hou Zheng-Guang for MoreLess, 2010

Silence dining chair
by Eason Qi for MoreLess, 2011

Silk stool
by Hou Zheng-Guang for MoreLess, 2009

Monk bench bookshelf
by Liu Yitong for MoreLess, 2010

PAINTING IN WOOD

Hou Zheng-Guang has designed a number of cabinets that incorporate an interesting and innovative technique whereby a pixelated landscape scene is mechanically carved into the wooden door panels and then picked out with 'ink'. The effect, when seen from a distance, is reminiscent of ancient Chinese scroll paintings; viewed close up, though, the patterning has a much more contemporary, almost digital aesthetic. Certainly, these pixelated landscapes create an interesting product-user interaction, as they can be seen more clearly the further away the viewer stands from them. Indeed, stand too close and the landscapes dissolve into a sea of seemingly random carved dots. These three cabinets testify to the technical and aesthetic innovation that can be found in the work of the New Chinese School, which, at its best, looks to the past in order to look forward. As Hou observes, 'Design is not groundless, there are no truly original designs. Innovation is a process to discover beauty … our mission is to extend tradition.'

<u>SOUTH MOUNTAIN SIDEBOARD</u>
by Hou Zheng-Guang
for MoreLess, 2012

<u>SOUTH MOUNTAIN SIDEBOARD</u>
by Hou Zheng-Guang
for MoreLess, 2012

<u>SOUTH MOUNTAIN CABINET</u>
by Hou Zheng-Guang
for MoreLess, 2012

IZEN + EXPOCASA FURNITURE

BOLDLY CONTEMPORARY STATEMENTS

The idea of expressing power and rank three-dimensionally has long been a feature of Chinese culture, and in terms of furniture design, this is expressed today with the well-known concept of the 'boss table', basically a large statement desk. Indeed, in most large companies the CEO has a commodious office where a boss table is the centrepiece. It is a furniture item that is meant to impress and signify the elevated status of its occupant, but it is also a nod to Chinese scholar culture. In fact, this type of desk will often have a special drawer for storing calligraphy paper, and scholar's accoutrements, such as brushes and viewing rocks, will be displayed on it. Here

we have two very different contemporary interpretations of the boss table: the minimalist-style Zhao desk by IZEN, with its visually strong, almost architectural presence and bold symmetrical silhouette, and the Trident desk by Expocasa Furniture, which has a more dynamic feeling, with its asymmetrical layout and four-sectioned top. The other designs shown here similarly reflect the growing design confidence of Chinese furniture companies, with their clever contemporary riffs on oriental forms and motifs. And while these designs are primarily intended for the *huaren* market, they could easily have broader international appeal too.

↑
<u>Trident desk</u>
by Dong Hesu & Li Nan
for Expocasa Furniture, 2017

→
<u>Max chair</u>
by Dong Hesu & Li Nan
for Expocasa Furniture, 2018

→
70° COFFEE TABLE
by Dong Hcsu & Li Nan
for Expocasa Furniture, 2018

↓
SU ARMCHAIRS AND TABLES
by Tao Jincheng for IZEN, 2018

↓↓
ZHAO DESK AND ARMCHAIR
by Tao Jincheng for IZEN, 2018

JAMY YANG + LIU JIANG

PLAYING WITH FORM

Jamy Yang is an award-winning industrial designer and design strategist. He is also a design collector, who has his own private museum of industrial design in Shanghai. After studying at Zhejiang University and the China Academy of Art, he went to Germany to take a master's degree in industrial design on a full scholarship provided by the WK Foundation. He subsequently worked as a product designer for Siemens, before eventually returning to China and setting up his own agency, Yang Design, in 2005. He has since worked for various international design-led brands, including Absolut, Audi, Peugeot, Sigg, Tumi and Victorinox, and alongside this has championed the cause of design sustainability in China. His Yang House armchair, with its eye-catching faceted seat shell, is a contemporary exploration of Chinese mortise and tenon joinery, while his screen-incorporating light is a stunningly evocative three-dimensional deconstruction of a Chinese painting. Liu Jiang, although from a more traditional handicraft background, has similarly translated age-old Chinese forms and joinery techniques into something refreshingly contemporary. His Neo-Ming armchair and his Jumping Fish side chair are, like Jamy's designs, representative of the very broad stylistic scope of New Chinese Design.

CONSTRUCTIVE
CRAFT SIMPLICITY

One of China's most respected educators, Jiang Li is professor of furniture design at the Central Academy of Fine Arts in Beijing. One of her most important initiatives was to set up the annual 'Design for Sitting' exhibition in 2002, and every year since then, all the students on her course have been charged with designing their own chairs. Encouraged to experiment and innovate, they have so far produced designs that are outstandingly diverse. It is thanks to Professor Jiang and other enlightened design educators in China that the phrase 'Designed in China' is gaining ever-greater currency and gradually supplanting the 'Made in China' label. In fact, she believes that 'in the near future, Chinese designers will have to step up to the challenges of playing on the world stage', so she does her utmost to equip her students with the skills to do just that. But more than this, she also creates her own furniture designs, most notably her trio of Horse Rider straddle seats made of woven rattan, which intentionally evoke the feeling of sitting in a saddle. Her Nest saddle stool, also made of rattan, similarly reflects her interest in using sustainable natural materials and craft-based methods of manufacture in innovative ways. A similar handcrafted simplicity can also be found in the solid wood children's furniture created by Goo Design. By using traditional pinned mortise and tenon joints, which are very strong, Goo Design's furniture, including these diminutive chairs, is very easy to assemble from flat-pack, thus making it ideal for selling online. Both Jiang Li's and Goo Design's work demonstrates that innovation in design does not necessarily have to rely on high-tech methods of production, but can instead be achieved through the thoughtful application of craft-based ingenuity.

KUKA HOME

CHINESE CONTEMPORARY MAINSTREAM

One of the best-known and fastest growing Chinese-owned furniture brands, Kuka Home has over 4,500 exclusive stores and sells its designs in around 120 countries and regions. It boasts an extensive product line that increasingly reflects the new contemporary spirit emerging in China's design and manufacturing mainstream. Certainly, tastes are rapidly changing in China with younger buyers wanting ever more premium-quality furniture that is better in tune with their modern lifestyles – and this is exactly what Kuka Home specializes in. The Kuka Group, which owns Kuka Home as well as various other furniture brands, evolved from the Kuka Workshop established by Gu Yuhua in Nantong, Jiangsu Province in 1982. This enterprise, which was inspired by the legacy of Tiantai craftsmanship, focused on improving sofa-making techniques and, that same year, launched its popular Casual sofa range. In 1996, the Hangzhou Hailong Furniture Co. was established, which four years later participated for the first time at Furniture China expo in Shanghai, helping the venture to extend its international client base. In June 2003, the Kuka Craft brand was officially founded and two years later exhibited internationally for the first time at imm Cologne in Germany. That same year, Kuka also began a collaboration with the Italian-based sofa specialist, Calia Italia. In order to keep up with Kuka's sales growth, they opened in 2005 a large production facility in Xiasha, Hangzhou, boasting an area of 164,500 m² (1,770,663 ft²) and then an additional manufactory was opened in Zhenjiang in 2006. The following year the high-end Kuka Home leather sofa range was introduced, and a dedicated store was opened in Holland, heralding the increasing internationalization of the Kuka brand. Also in 2007, Kuka won the contract to supply seating for Air China's T3 Terminal (Section A) as part of the 2008 Beijing Summer Olympic Games project. Rapid expansion ensued and in 2011 Kuka Home Co. was officially founded. The firm showcased the world's first 3D-printed sofa in 2015, and the following year it was successfully listed on the Shanghai Stock Exchange. Since then, as part of a 'go out' strategy, it has purchased a majority shareholding in the Italian-brand Natuzzi, and also acquired the well-known German furniture brand Rolf Benz. As one of the most dominant players in the Chinese upholstered furnishings sector, Kuka Home has won numerous awards and is deeply committed to design innovation as its launch of the aforementioned 3D-printed sofa testifies. It is, however, the kind of stylish contemporary designs shown here that are its greatest strength, because they have a globally appealing functional practicality as well as an easy-to-live-with elegant aesthetic.

Model 2728 sofa
by Kuka design team
for Kuka Home, 2016

Model A1018 lounge chair
by Kuka design team
for Kuka Home, 2014

LAI YANAN + YU HONGQUAN/DOMO

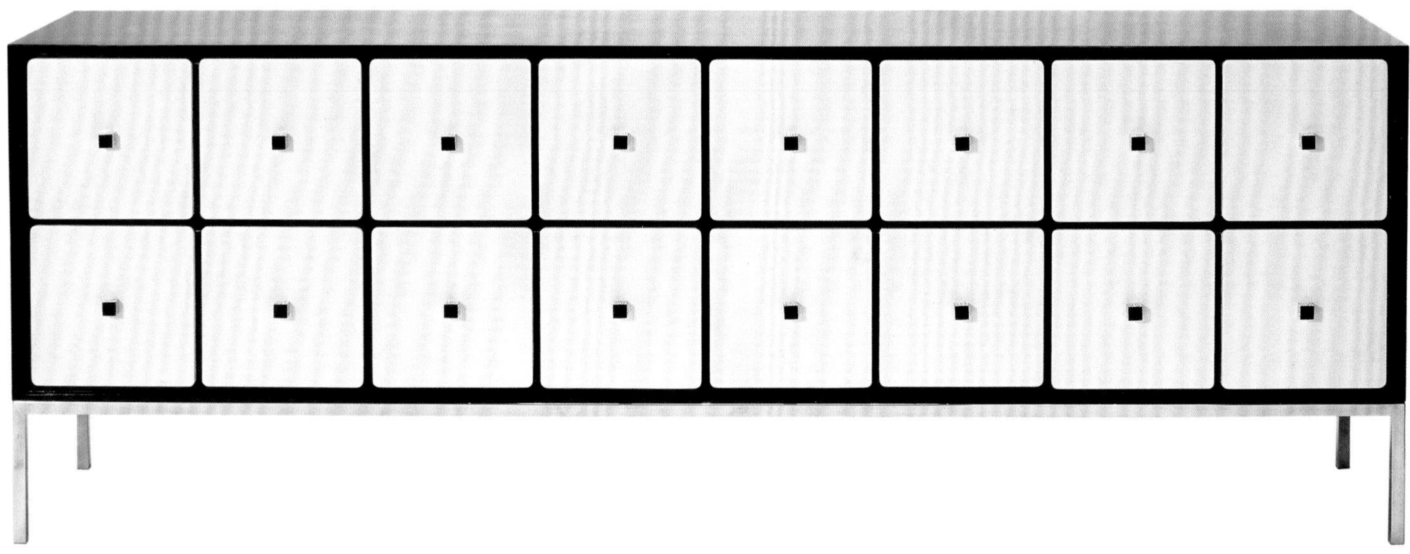

↑
<u>Eggshell lacquered sideboard with drawers</u>
by Lai Yanan and Yu Hongquan
for Domo Nature, 2006

↓
Details of square-shaped handle (left) and drawer
front (right) on Lai Yanan and Yu Hongquan's two
Eggshell lacquered sideboards, 2006

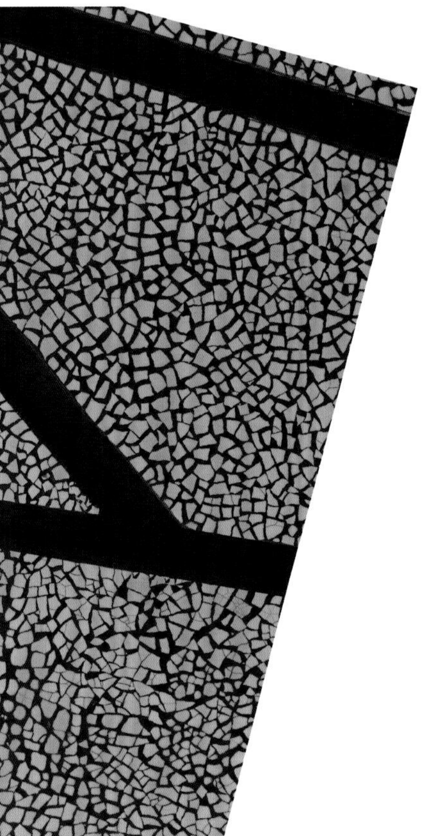

MODERN LACQUER

Lai Yanan and Yu Hongquan are among China's leading interior designers, and are well known for their people-orientated approach, which is intended to provide emotional comfort and a sense of well-being. In 2004 this husband-and-wife team founded Domo Nature, which has become one of China's most high-profile furniture and lifestyle brands. Not only an early proponent of New Chinese Design, it was also instrumental in introducing what Lai describes as 'the integrated system design concept' into China, by which she means conceiving their annual furniture collections within fully integrated interior contexts. Indeed, Domo's gallery-like showrooms, like those of most other furniture brands in China, are laid out as a series of themed rooms so that clients can buy a total look if they wish. The couple's interest in collecting antique Chinese furniture and artefacts constantly informs their vast range of contemporary designs. For instance, their 2006 furniture collection featured a series of beautiful eggshell lacquered pieces, shown here, that stylishly channelled a 1920s Shanghai Art Deco aesthetic.

Eggshell lacquered sideboard
by Lai Yanan and Yu Hongquan
for Domo Nature, 2006

Eggshell lacquered chest of drawers
by Lai Yanan and Yu Hongquan
for Domo Nature, 2006

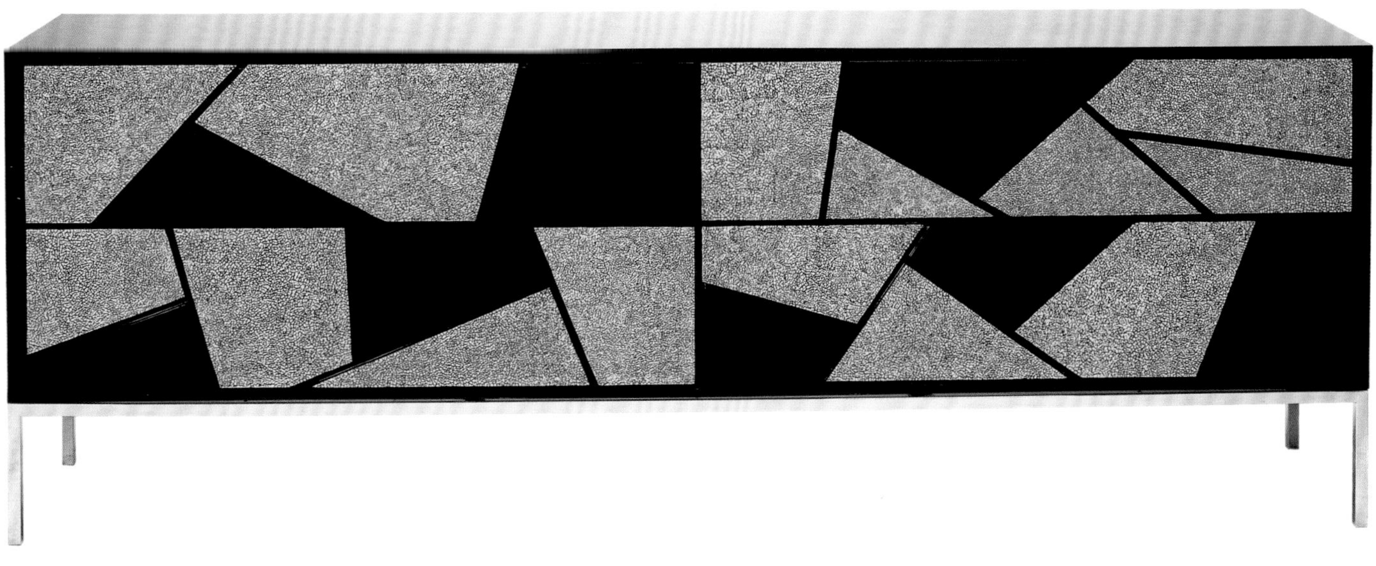

DESIGNS FOR OUTDOORS

Having found success with the Domo Nature brand, Lai Yanan and Yu Hongquan established a new sister brand in 2015. Known as Domo Life, it specializes in the design and manufacture of stylishly contemporary outdoor furniture. Among its most notable weather-resistant designs are the sculptural Pea chair, with its enveloping organic-form backrest, and the Mountain chair and sofa, which evoke the mountainous landscapes so often depicted in traditional Chinese painting. Through these designs, Lai and Yu want to convey the spirit of the natural world, for they believe that will allow people to connect with the furniture on a more emotional level. As they say, 'Design should reflect both the aesthetics of life and the philosophy of life … Design should touch and reflect the spiritual world.'

LI RUOFAN/LOST&FOUND

CHANNELLING
THE '30 YEARS' STYLE

Lost&Found is one of China's leading lifestyle brands, and was one of the first to champion the New Chinese Style. Li Ruofan, who is originally from southern China and initially made her name as a designer of accessories, founded the venture in 2008. Prior to this, she opened some of the first coffee shops in China in the late 1980s, ostensibly to showcase her designs alongside her growing collection of antiques, which included original anonymous furniture from the Soviet-influenced '30 Years' era (the period from Mao Zedong's Cultural Revolution to Deng Xiaoping's Economic Reforms). During the 1980s and 1990s Li was also highly influenced by Japanese lifestyle/ well-being culture, and this led her to begin collecting Japanese handicrafts, which she skilfully mixed into her coffee-shop interiors. Eventually, she moved into designing furniture that channelled the utilitarian 30 Years style. By 2008, when she opened her first Lost&Found showroom in Beijing, there was a growing nostalgia for this era, which reminded many people of the simpler lifestyles they had lost in the face of so much economic, cultural and social upheaval. In fact, the whole concept behind Lost&Found is to create furniture that has an innate purity and simplicity, and that offers unpretentious practicality and comfort in order to make people feel at home in their domestic surroundings.

→|
CHENXIANG BEDROOM CABINET
by Li Ruofan for Lost&Found, 2008

←
SHANGHAI IRON PIPE CHAIR
by Li Ruofan for Lost&Found, 2008

→|
STUDIO DESK
by Li Ruofan for Lost&Found, 2008

FAMILY BABY CHAIR
by Yue Xiao for Lost&Found, 2016 – specially
designed so that it can be used by infants from
six months to three years of age

SIMPLIFIED CHINESE

Lost&Found was one of the first independent furniture stores to open in China in the early twenty-first century. Its founder, Li Ruofan, is a devotee of 'slow-paced' design, and believes firmly that 'the home should look like a home, not a store'. The social aspect of furniture is very important to her, and through her 'quiet designs' she hopes to provide a sense of calm and emotional well-being. She prefers designs that are low-key and casual, and that almost disappear into the background because they are so unassuming. Her simple, unfussy designs, and those of her design team, are the antithesis of the showy 'tycoon' style, and she observes wryly that younger, less design-savvy clients often find her furniture 'too plain and want a more "designed" look'. The pieces shown here are typical of Lost&Found's simple yet chic Chinese aesthetic, each referencing ancient Ming forms in a very pared-down way, but beautifully crafted and detailed. Yue Xiao's Qijia armchair, for example, takes the simplified form of a Ming design known as the Horseshoe Chair because of the shape of its top rail.

← **QIJIA TEA SHELVED CABINET**
by Yue Xiao for Lost&Found, 2012

↓ **QIJIA ARMCHAIR**
by Yue Xiao for Lost&Found, 2012

↓↓ **QIJIA STUDY DESK**
by Yue Xiao for Lost&Found, 2012

CHINESE UTILITY

The founder of Lost&Found, Li Ruofan, spends a lot of time thinking about the functionality of furniture, as well as its role in our daily lives. As she notes, 'The burden of life is enough, so I want to provide people with simple and beautiful furniture, clean and neat. Life should be like this, simply simple.' Consequently, many of Lost&Found's designs created by Li and her in-house team of designers are inspired by the everyday anonymous designs of the past. The firm's Normal range of furniture, which includes the bookcase shown here, exemplifies the straightforward simplicity and functional flexibility that she seeks. The cabinets from the Normal range are based on the concept of modularity, with each element functioning like a building block that can be combined with others to create a host of different bedside tables, bookcases and television cabinets. Zhao Muyi's At Your Pleasure tea table is also noteworthy for its functional adaptability. It has a hinged, 'old-fashioned' basin frame, which is simple and stable, and is also easy to take apart and transport. The design's height of 37cm (14½in) was also carefully considered so that it could work as a tea table when used in conjunction with chairs or sofas, but could also be used to eat at while sitting crossed-legged on the floor. The At Your Pleasure trolley/side table, also by Zhao, is likewise highly adaptable: the tabletop can be used as a tray, while the hinged mobile frame can be easily collapsed when not in use. It is the Moonlike dressing table, however, that probably best exemplifies the Lost&Found aesthetic, which 'must be an everyday, quiet and beautiful presence'.

↑
NORMAL SHELF
by Chi Shuaishuai for Lost&Found, 2017

→
MOONLIKE DRESSER
by Zhao Muyi for Lost&Found, 2016

↑↑
Detail of the Moonlike dresser

↑
The top of the At Your Pleasure tea
table being used as a serving tray

AT YOUR PLEASURE SIDE TABLE
by Zhao Muyi for Lost&Found, 2016

↓
AT YOUR PLEASURE TEA TABLE
by Zhao Muyi for Lost&Found, 2016

JUDY LO (LO YU-FEN)

STOOLS RETHOUGHT

The Taipei-based designer Judy Lo, like so many Chinese-speaking designers, also goes by her Chinese birth name, Lo Yu-Fen. She studied industrial design at Shih Chien University in Taipei, and is one of the very few female designers from the *huaren* community to have made a name in the still male-dominated world of design. She is the creative director of the design company Pinyen Creative and was named a Rising Asian Talent at the 2014 Maison & Objet in Paris, the very first designer based in the Taiwan region to receive this accolade. She specializes in producing modern designs that are informed by local culture, materials and craftsmanship. Most of her designs incorporate the natural wonder material bamboo, which is not particularly surprising, given the long bamboo-weaving traditions existing locally. Lo is best known for her Ru-Ju stool, which was debuted at the London Design Festival in 2012. The design's form is based on the shape of an ancient jade coin. Its seat section is a smooth, doughnut-like circle of solid wood that is warm to the touch and surprisingly comfortable to sit on. The stool's legs, ingeniously made from ribbon-like

bands of bent bamboo, support this circle of solid wood and, although delicate in appearance, are surprisingly resilient. The overall effect is that the stool's seat seems to hover, as if defying the laws of gravity, and is being held in place only by the anchoring loops of bamboo. Lo's Tutu stool/tea table is also made of bamboo and is equally innovative. This interesting, multifunctional design incorporates three tubes made from open-work woven bamboo that function as legs and support a tray-like wooden top into which a circular cushion can be slotted. Its remarkable visual lightness is a tribute to Lo's clever exploitation of bamboo's extraordinarily high strength-to-weight ratio.

↑ & →|
RU-JU STOOL
by Judy Lo (self-production), 2011
– executed with the assistance
of Natou artisan Chen Gao-Ming

↙
TUTU STOOL
by Judy Lo for Pin-Collection/Pinyen Creative,
2013 – executed with the assistance
of Natou artisan Su Suren

LV YONGZHONG/BANMOO

CULTURAL INFLUENCES

The architect/designer Lv Yongzhong established his own furniture and life-style brand, Banmoo, in 2006 with the aim of 'seeking tranquillity in urban life', and certainly his designs have a highly restrained aesthetic that evokes a sense of calm. The name 'Banmoo' is a compound of two Chinese words, *ban* meaning 'halfness' and symbolizing the quest to strike a balance between utility and spirituality as it relates to Taoism, and *moo* meaning 'wood', which not only refers to the material used for most of his designs, but also, as Lv puts it, to 'forms which contain the origin of natural life'. Many of his designs also reference Chinese cultural influences. For example, his well-known Suzhou armchair was inspired by the arching form of the Feng Bridge that spans the Suzhou section of the Grand Canal, as well as the graceful lines found in the layouts and structure of that city's various historic gardens. The undulating form of his stunning Seven String table is, by contrast, evolved from a very specific type of table used to hold the ancient seven-stringed instrument known as a *qin*, while its exquisitely contoured profile was inspired by the flowing lines of costumes worn during the Han dynasty. Many of Lv's other designs 'seek peacefulness and serenity' by channelling furniture forms associated more with the Ming dynasty, which represented the zenith of historical Chinese furniture design and manufacture. As he notes, 'From ancient to modern China, I think there is a need to connect with the past that we used to have, with the atmosphere, and the people and the crafts that we once enjoyed.' Indeed, it could be said that the New Chinese Style, of which Banmoo's designs are so representative, is in fact a renaissance design movement.

SEVEN STRING TABLE
by Lv Yongzhong for Banmoo, 2012 – on it is a flute-shaped incense burner, which was Lv Yongzhong's very first design, dating from 2000

OCTANGLE ROUND-BACKED ARMCHAIR WITH SONG LUOHAN COUCH AND ANHUI SCREEN in the foyer of the Banmoo Gallery in Beijing, opened 2014

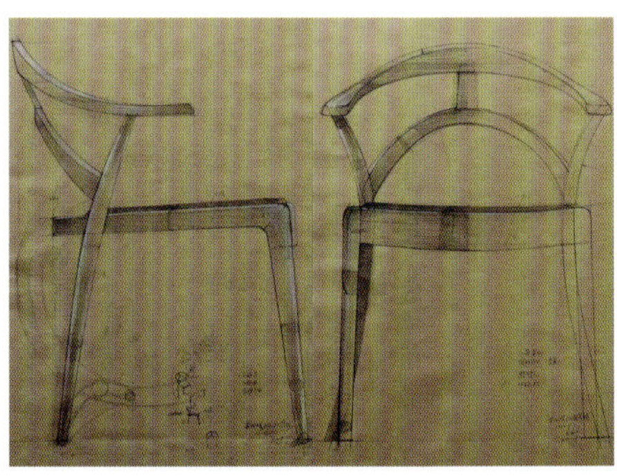

SUZHOU ARMCHAIR
by Lv Yongzhong for Banmoo, 2011

DESIGN AS INTEGRATED LIFESTYLE

In China, interior designers are held in the same high regard as architects, and successful ones often become celebrities. One of China's most highly respected interior designers is Lv Yongzhong, who studied architecture at the renowned Tongji University in Shanghai, then spent another 20 years working there as a lecturer. During this time he also worked extensively as an interior designer, winning numerous awards for his various *feng shui*-based interior schemes. In 2006 Lv (pronounced 'lu') branched out by founding his own company, Banmoo, which has become one of the most high-profile furniture and lifestyle brands in China. Like many designers working there, Lv conceives his designs mostly in the context of a fully integrated room setting, because in China many people, whether professional specifiers buying for clients or private customers acquiring designs for their own homes, purchase a complete interior look straight from the showroom. The success of Lv's work lies in his ability to reference Chinese traditions and craft, but in a very contemporary way that is suited to modern living.

↗
HORIZON TABLE, BENCH AND
CABINET WITH SUZHOU CHAIRS
IN AN INTERIOR SETTING
by Lv Yongzhong for Banmoo, 2011

⇥
ANHUI EMPEROR CHAIR AND
CALLIGRAPHY TABLE
by Lv Yongzhong for Banmoo, 2012 –
shown in Banmoo's Beijing gallery

← & →
ESSENCE SCREEN
by Lv Yongzhong for Banmoo, 2005

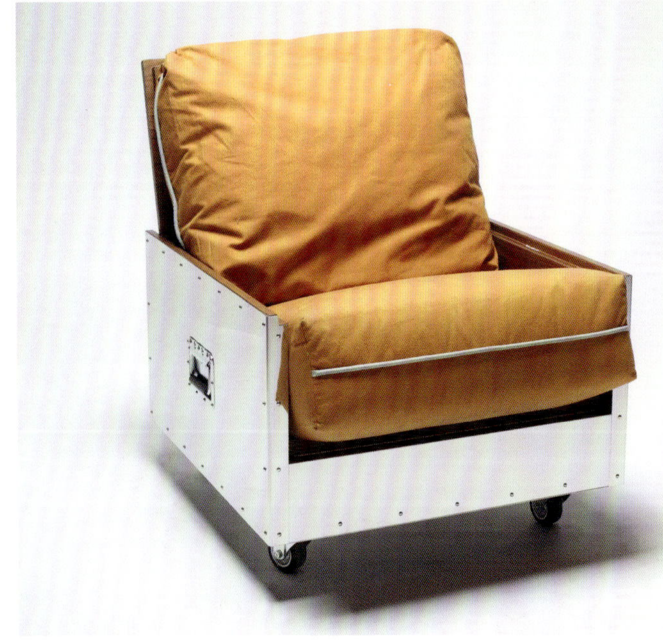

THINKING INSIDE THE BOX

The Chinese architect-designer Li Naihan studied at the Bartlett School of Architecture in London before working as the project coordinator for the Jinhua Architecture Park project, which commenced in 2002 and was curated by the Chinese artist Ai Weiwei. She subsequently co-founded BAO Atelier and began working on various interior, exhibition and graphic-design projects. In 2010 she exhibited her first furniture designs at the Salone del Mobile in Milan, and while she was unpacking these pieces on their return to Beijing in shipping crates, she got the inspiration for her Crates series. The first iteration of this pop-up series debuted at Beijing Design Week in 2011 and comprised various mobile wooden storage boxes that, when opened up, revealed folding sofas and beds, as well as dressing tables, kitchens, wardrobes and even a table-football table. Inspired by Beijing's rapidly shifting urban landscape, this collection was all about taking design thinking inside the box. It was subsequently nominated for the 2012 Design of the Year Awards, organized by the Design Museum in London. Two years later Gallery ALL commissioned Li to design these black walnut and stainless steel versions of her metamorphic Crates, which have a far less rough-and-ready look than her earlier pieces, but are no less intriguing.

THE CLOTH VALET STORAGE CLOSET
FROM THE CRATE SERIES
by Li Naihan for Gallery ALL, 2014

THE SPACE CLOSET
+ THE MONUMENT

In many ways Li Naihan's Crate collection can be regarded as more of a lifestyle concept than a range of furniture per se. Inspired initially by shipping containers, these clever metamorphic designs are perfectly attuned to the nomadic nature of contemporary life, and reflect the remarkable shifting population trends that have been witnessed in cities across China over the last 20 years or so. The concept of dwelling in a fast-moving, mobile world fascinates Li, and her Crate designs are ultimately responses to this idea. As she observes, 'All my creations are designed to improve the life I'm living right now. To do that you need to understand what life is about. It's a process.' Her contemporaneous I Am a Monument series takes the scaled-down forms of famous landmark buildings and turns them into usable furniture. The idea behind these pieces was inspired by the legend that an emperor during the Han dynasty had re-created in miniature China's entire landmass out of bonsai trees. Like Li's Crate series, these architecture-inspired furniture pieces have a revelatory Chinese puzzle-box quality, which is surprisingly delightful and delightfully surprising.

CCTV BUILDING WARDROBE
FROM I AM A MONUMENT SERIES
by Li Naihan for Gallery ALL, 2014

TABLES OF INTEREST

The Taipei-based designer Pili Wu is best known for his Plastic Classic chair, which he designed as a student in 2008, and which became one of the most celebrated Chinese furniture designs of the decade. Similarly thought-provoking and inventive, his Marble Weaving tables, designed nearly a decade later, cleverly use the off-cuts left from marble processing. Pili takes these 'waste' stones and uses water-jets to cut them into precisely calculated shapes, which he assembles into traditional bamboo-weaving patterns specific to the Taiwan region. He then uses these to make the tops of his tables. By doing this, Pili not only transforms unwanted waste into beautiful objects with both aesthetic and functional value, but is also able 'to convey the unique local marble culture'. Li Naihan's Mother Butterfly folding table, which is made from two very different materials – rosewood and acrylic – likewise makes overt reference to indigenous local culture, with the beautiful and complex pattern of its inlay being devised by a folk paper-cutting artist from Guiyang. This striking decorative device references the well-known Butterfly Mother folk tale, which is derived from the age-old creation myth of the Miao people from the Guizhou region of southern China.

MOTHER BUTTERFLY TABLE
FROM THE FOLD SERIES
by Li Naihan
for Gallery ALL, 2014

Marble weaving tables
by Pili Wu for Studio Shikai, 2017

Detail of Marble Weaving tables

MA CONG

EMBROIDERED LANDSCAPES

Ma Cong is the founder and creative director of Hundredicrafts, a cultural heritage and handicraft platform that seeks to encourage innovation in contemporary Chinese handcraft-based design. But more than this, he is also a highly skilled designer-craftsman in his own right, having won a gold Bai Hua medal, which is only ever awarded to China's most accomplished arts and crafts masters. Such is his standing that Ma Cong was also the first-ever Chinese designer to be invited to stage a solo show at Milan's famous Triennale Building. Indeed, he is one of China's great embroidery specialists, creating stunning screens with modern abstract patterns that employ a painstaking dual-sided embroidery technique, which was widely used during the Ming and Qing dynasties. The frames of his delicate embroidered silk gauze floor screens are constructed of Burmese padauk wood, using traditional mortise and tenon joints. The exquisite dual-sided embroidered motif of The Running Cloud screen is inspired by representations of clouds and rivers found in Chinese ink paintings. That of The Golden Faith screen is likewise an abstracted and stylized representation of water and clouds, but it is also intended to reveal the poetic beauty and spiritually uplifting brilliance of light in all its glowing glory.

→|
THE GOLDEN FAITH SCREEN
by Ma Cong (self-production), 2015

←
Detail of The Running Cloud screen, showing its exquisite stitching

→|
THE RUNNING CLOUD SCREEN
by Ma Cong (self-production), 2016

MA YANSONG/MAD

INTERPLANETARY DESIGN VISIONS

Internationally acknowledged as one of the greatest creative pioneers of his generation, Ma Yangsong is not only the most influential Chinese architect working today, but a formidably talented designer too. Born in Beijing, he initially studied at Beijing Institute of Civil Engineering and Architecture, then took a masters degree in architecture at Yale University in the USA, before founding MAD Architects in 2004.

The practice has since become renowned for its breathtakingly avant-garde buildings and urban plans that seek a balance 'between humanity, the city and the environment'. In 2012 Ma's visionary approach was spectacularly showcased in his concept scheme for Shanshui City, an ultra-modern urban development of 'mountains and water' proposed for Guiyang. This project helped to solidify his reputation abroad, and two years later MAD became the first Chinese architecture practice to win a competition to design a landmark cultural project overseas: the Lucas Museum of Narrative Art in Chicago. Since then Ma, like other architects who use digital parametric tools to develop their designs for buildings, has broadened his remit into the world of limited-edition furniture. In 2015 Yu Wang, the co-founder and director of Galley ALL, commissioned him to create a series of design-art pieces on the theme of MAD Martian – in other words, how the furniture of Chinese interplanetary colonizers might look. The resulting otherworldly 'hybrid' designs, made using a combination of advanced robotic manufacturing and artisanal skills, are meant to reflect the inspirational impact of the Martian landscape on these imagined space pioneers, as well as their inevitable nostalgia for their home planet Earth.

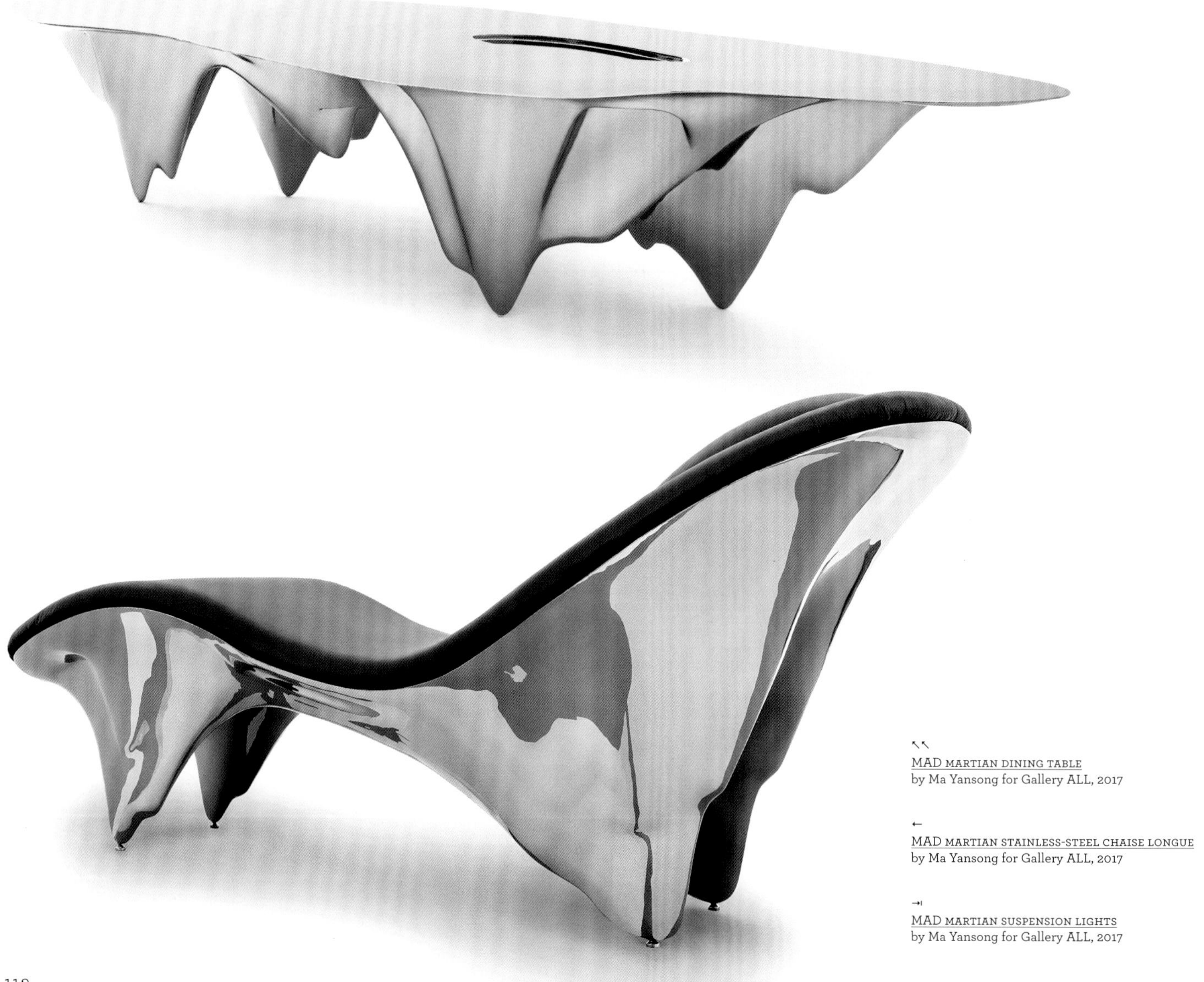

↖↖
MAD MARTIAN DINING TABLE
by Ma Yansong for Gallery ALL, 2017

←
MAD MARTIAN STAINLESS-STEEL CHAISE LONGUE
by Ma Yansong for Gallery ALL, 2017

→|
MAD MARTIAN SUSPENSION LIGHTS
by Ma Yansong for Gallery ALL, 2017

NERI&HU

CRAFT-INSPIRED DESIGNS

Neri&Hu Design and Research Office was founded in 2004 by the architects Lyndon Neri and Rossana Hu. The partnership has since forged a formidable reputation as one of China's most innovative interdisciplinary architecture and design practices. In terms of their product design output, the partners have tended to focus on furniture and lighting. For example, they have designed a number of highly inventive pieces for Stellar Works, most notably the Ming chair, with its distinctive arching profile. Their Dowry Cabinet III for Stellar Works and Commune table for De La Espada likewise explore the potential of traditional Chinese forms and typologies, while exploiting the innate beauty of natural materials and the inherent value of high-quality craftsmanship. Their Solo chair is slightly different in that its figure-cradling seat form was originally inspired by an Eames Plastic Shell chair, but it nonetheless projects a very elegant oriental aesthetic.

↑
Ming chair
by Neri&Hu for Stellar Works,
2016

←
Dowry cabinet III
by Neri&Hu for Stellar Works,
2016

SOLO DINING CHAIR
by Neri&Hu (in collaboration
with De La Espada), 2008

COMMUNE COFFEE TABLE
by Neri&Hu (in collaboration
with De La Espada), 2016

NEW INTERPRETATIONS

The Neri&Hu partnership works on projects across the world, ranging from architecture and interior-design commissions to product design and graphic communication. Over the years it has also devised various eye-catching exhibition installations. Its founders, Lyndon Neri and Rossana Hu, see design as a potent channel for explorative investigation, and as a result their furniture designs are often very innovative in their use of materials and construction, as well as in form and function. Their Lan collection, for example, reimagines the traditional living room by breaking down its constituent parts, with the seating units and matching rug providing an integrated spatial composition that references the form of a traditional weaving loom as well as textile bales. This is a nod to the fact that its manufacturer is better known for its production of woven textiles. By contrast, their Cabinet of Curiosity was inspired by the trolley carts used in ceramics factories, hence the design's stripped-back, form-follows-function purity. The duo's Hanger coat stand, with its rounded rectangular frame of tubular steel adorned with simple leather straps and set on a concrete base, has a similar minimalist aesthetic that seeks to find the perfect balance between the utilitarian and the domestic.

↓
LAN COLLECTION
by Neri&Hu for Gan, 2018

←
CABINET OF CURIOSITY
by Neri&Hu for Stellar Works, 2015

↓
HANGER COAT STAND
by Neri&Hu for Offecct, 2016

NEO-CHINESE

The Kuka Group is one of the largest players within the contemporary Chinese home-furnishing sector. It comprises various lifestyle brands that manufacture and retail widely different styles of furniture, including Orient Casa. This venture is interesting because it has fully embraced the spirit of New Chinese Design, and many of its products strike a good balance between tradition and modernity. The company's beautiful Mural screen, Void armchair and Third urn-shaped stool, although making obvious reference to historic furniture antecedents, also have a practicality that is suited to modern life. As in so many contemporary Chinese furniture designs, the materials used in their construction, whether marble, rosewood, silk or leather, are showcased to best advantage. A devotion to 'luxury materials' continues to this day, but there is also an increasing trend towards assessing furniture as much by the quality of its design as the materials it is made of. This is an interesting development, and one that is bound to expand even further given the new crop of young Chinese designers

who are powerfully demonstrating that good design is in itself a highly valuable commodity. In fact, good design is a holistic approach to problem-solving, and by its very nature encompasses thoughtful material choices and ethical production values, as well as timeless aesthetics and enduring functionality.

↑
THIRD STOOL
by Chen Ruoyu
for Orient Casa, 2014

↖
FIRST STOOL
by Chen Ruoyu
for Orient Casa, 2014

←
VOID CHAIR
by Chen Ruoyu and Wang Shichao
for Orient Casa, 2016

→
CLOUDS COFFEE TABLE
by Chen Ruoyu
for Orient Casa, 2014

↓
MURAL SCREEN
by Chen Ruoyu and Chen Da
for Orient Casa, 2016

AVA ARMCHAIR
by Song Wen Zhong
for Roche Bobois, 2009

→|
SLIDING TEA TABLE
by People's Industrial Design Office
(self-production), 2014 – three views

NEW CHINESE DESIGN HORIZONS

The design team at People's Industrial Design Office (PIDO) is well known for its innovative furniture designs, intended mainly for office environments. It has even created a modular office tabling system based on forms inspired by the tile-matching video game Tetris. This talented team has also designed the stunning sliding table shown here, which is made of both stainless steel and galvanized steel, and again intended for office use. This unusual tea table has a strong sculptural presence reminiscent of the minimalist 1970s sculptures by the American artist Carl Andre. It is fabricated from eight triangular metal sections – five of galvanized steel for the static base, and three of satin-finished stainless steel for the tabletop surface. Furthermore, the latter are able to slide, providing an interesting element of interactivity and multifunctionality. The tea table and the tea-drinking rituals that take place around it are very important within the Chinese business community, being a means of building trust between potential collaborators. While PIDO's tables have a weighty visual mass, Song Wen Zhong's Ava chair for Roche Bobois, on the other hand, has an ethereal visual lightness. This remarkable polycarbonate chair was created for, and then won, the Roche Bobois Design Award in 2009, when the theme of the competition was 'Nature, a Universal Link between Occident and Orient'. The technologically advanced gas-injection moulding process used in its production is much more eco-efficient than traditional plastic-moulding techniques because it uses less energy and less material. Also, because the Ava chair is made entirely of polycarbonate, it is eminently recyclable. Its fluid form was inspired by Chinese myths about shape-shifting dragons, and also by the elegant curvilinear forms of Ming furniture.

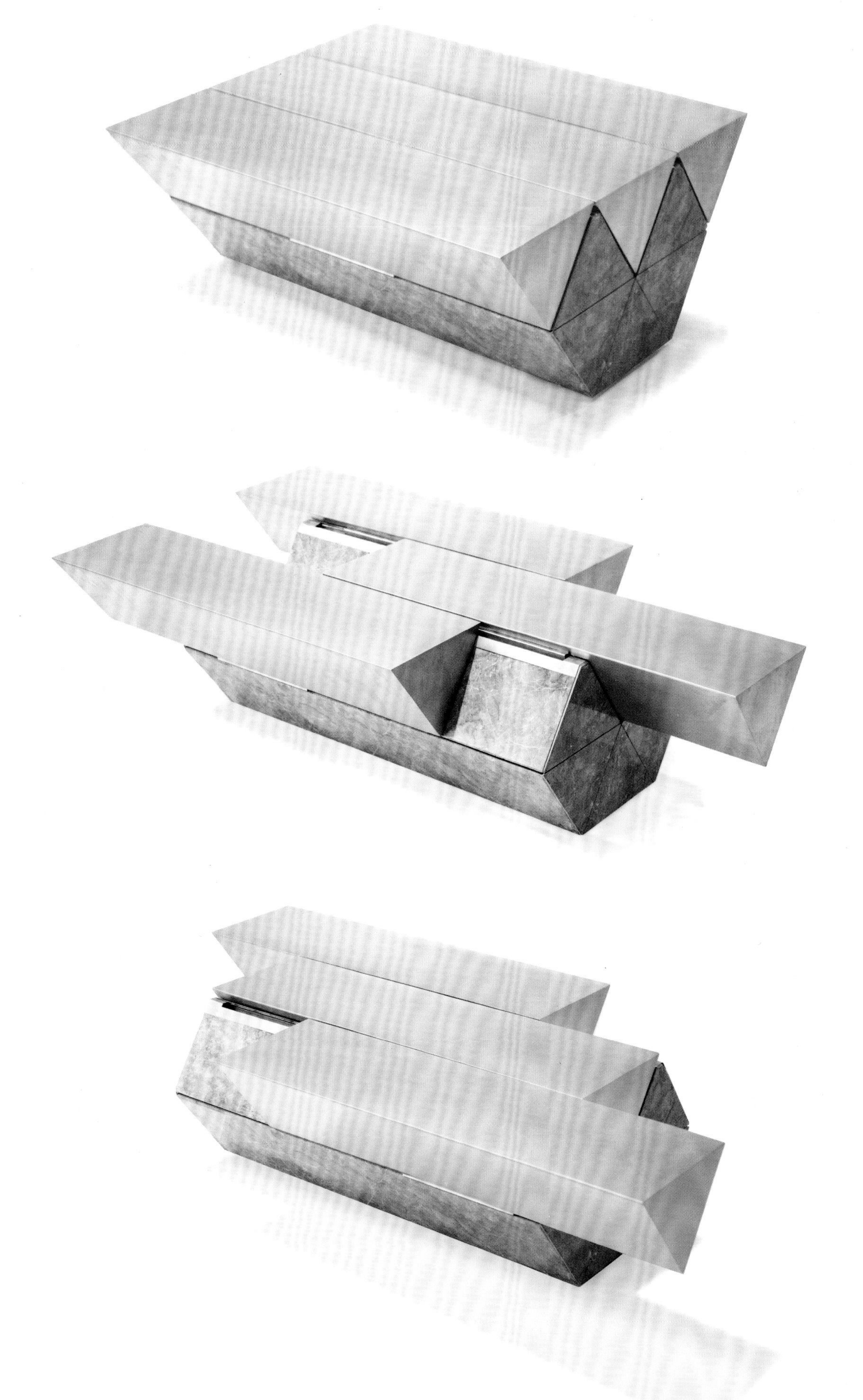

PEOPLE'S INDUSTRIAL DESIGN OFFICE

CLEVERLY WIRED SOLUTIONS

He Zhe, James Shen and Zang Feng founded the People's Industrial Design Office (PIDO) in Beijing in 2010, the same year they established a sister architecture practice, People's Architecture Office. Over the intervening period PIDO has gained an international reputation for designing innovative furnishing solutions that have mainly contract and office application. The Mesh chair, with its stripped-back wire-rod construction, is a perfect example of the studio's thoughtful essentialist approach to design. Its development was ultimately an exercise in efficiency, with a single bent and twisted metal rod forming its frame.

The diagonal hatching of thinner-gauge steel wires that make up the chair's seat and back has large gaps in it where material is not strictly needed for constructional integrity. The earlier Mesh outdoor collection, which includes a double-seater sofa, an armchair and a coffee table, likewise uses wire rods to materially efficient ends and to spectacular optical effect. The sofa and chair's strict geometric bases rise into curvilinear criss-crossed grids of epoxy-coated steel wire rods that follow the contours of the human body to provide as much comfort as possible with the minimum of means.

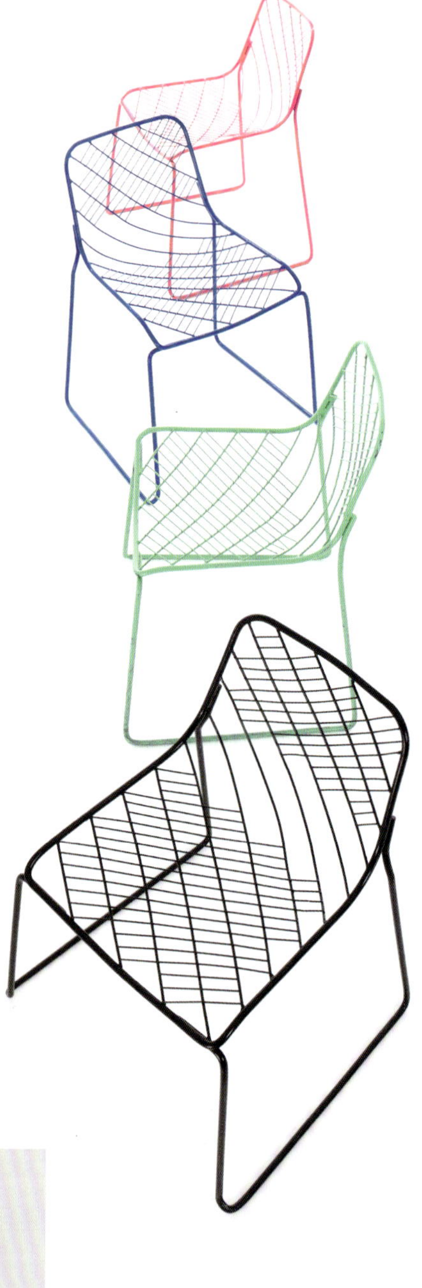

MESH CHAIRS
by People's Industrial Design Office, 2017

MESH ARMCHAIR FOR OUTDOOR USE
by People's Industrial Design Office, 2013

MESH SOFA FOR OUTDOOR USE
by People's Industrial Design Office, 2013

Detail of Mesh sofa
by People's Industrial Design Office, 2013

MELDING THE PAST WITH
THE PRESENT

The Taipei-based designer Pili Wu created his Plastic Classic chair when he was still a student at college in 2008. While undertaking research for his final project, he felt there was a cultural disconnect between the Ming furniture forms of the past and what he was experiencing in his own everyday life. Looking to the streets of Taipei for inspiration, he noticed the prevalence of a simple, anonymously designed plastic stool. As he explains, 'In the Taiwan region, plastic stools are very popular; they can be seen on streets and [in] alleys, and are used at … food stalls and *ban dou* [traditional outdoor banquets for weddings and suchlike]. This island used to be a plastic production kingdom, so plastic chairs and stools have been present in our daily lives for a very long time, yet interestingly, nobody knows about the designer of this well-known plastic stool.' Thanks to its simple form, it is easy to mass-produce at a very low cost, which has no doubt contributed to its popularity. Yet, as Pili observes, although it was so ubiquitous in the local island culture, no one ever really noticed it. He therefore made a wooden chair that had a base inspired by this modern icon, while its arms and back channelled classical Ming forms. This interesting hybrid design was an early and influential example of New Chinese Design, and has become an acknowledged contemporary classic. A later, lacquered version was also made.

←
<u>PLASTIC CLASSIC CHAIR</u>
by Pili Wu for Han Gallery, 2008

→
Plastic Classic shown alongside the anonymously designed, mass-produced plastic stool that inspired its creation

↑ & ←
<u>PIAO ARMCHAIR</u>
by Pinwu (self-production), 2010

EXPERIMENTS IN MATERIALITY

Based in Hangzhou, the Pinwu design studio was founded by three young designers with very different backgrounds, but who shared the goal of revitalizing ancient Chinese craft traditions by incorporating them into innovative contemporary designs. This talented trio is made up of the Chinese product designer Zhang Lei, the German furniture and automotive designer Christoph John, and the Serbian furniture and interior designer Jovana Bogdanovic. Among their most notable furniture designs are the Bing bookcase, which is made from Chinese pine and inspired by the ice-like patterns traditionally used on Chinese window screens. Adding extra sections, which are secured with specially designed metal connectors, the bookcase can be endlessly extended. The Piao armchair, by contrast, takes its inspiration from paper umbrellas, which have long been made in the ancient city of Hangzhou. Sitting atop a beechwood frame, the chair's shell-like seating section is made by glueing thin layers of rice paper together in exactly the same way used for making umbrellas. By employing this lamination method and then moulding it into the required form, the layers of paper eventually become strong and stable enough to sit on, yet retain an inherent flexibility thanks to the interwoven nature of the paper's natural fibres. Pinwu's Run tables reference another major Chinese craft: porcelain manufacture. As its designers explain, 'The durability and sturdiness of porcelain make it an ideal table-top surface.' Available in a range of attractive colours and sizes, and twinned with simple beechwood legs, Pinwu's porcelain tables have an endearing retro aesthetic that provides a tangible sense of warmth and domesticity in any interior.

↑
<u>Run tables</u>
by Pinwu (self-production), 2012

→
<u>Bing bookcase</u>
by Pinwu (self-production), 2014

QIU SIMIN/QIU

CELEBRATING IMPERFECTION

The predictability of perfection can be quite boring, especially in industrially manufactured products, so it is refreshing to find a number of Chinese designers whose work celebrates the joys of imperfection. One such designer is Qiu Simin, who studied product design at London's Royal College of Art. While there, he created an innovative eco-friendly tap that made water flow in a swirling vortex, thereby achieving a 15 per cent reduction in water usage. Since his return to China, he has continued to think about sustainability, especially in relation to the production of rosewood furniture. As he notes, 'The preciousness of the wood and the delicacy of the carving have always been the attributes that the rosewood furniture industry has been proud of. But can the replication of styles from the Ming and Qing dynasties or in the "New Chinese Design" style really bring the industry within the reaches of sustainable development?' With this in mind, Qiu has sought a more sustainable approach to working with rosewood. Generally, only the dense and finely grained core of a rosewood log is used for furniture; the outer layers are discarded because of their imperfections, such as hollows, wormholes, surface scrapes and colour variations. For Qiu, however, this rejected timber is 'full of poetry and beauty that is uniquely created by nature'. Indeed, his Imperfection range of furniture quirkily celebrates the remarkable variety of colours and irregular forms found in leftover timber, which has historically been treated as almost worthless by-products of the Chinese rosewood furniture industry.

IMPERFECTION BENCH
by Qiu Simin for Qiu, 2018

↓ & →
IMPERFECTION STOOL
by Qiu Simin for Qiu, 2018

↓↓
IMPERFECTION COAT STAND
by Qiu Simin for Qiu, 2018

SHANG XIA

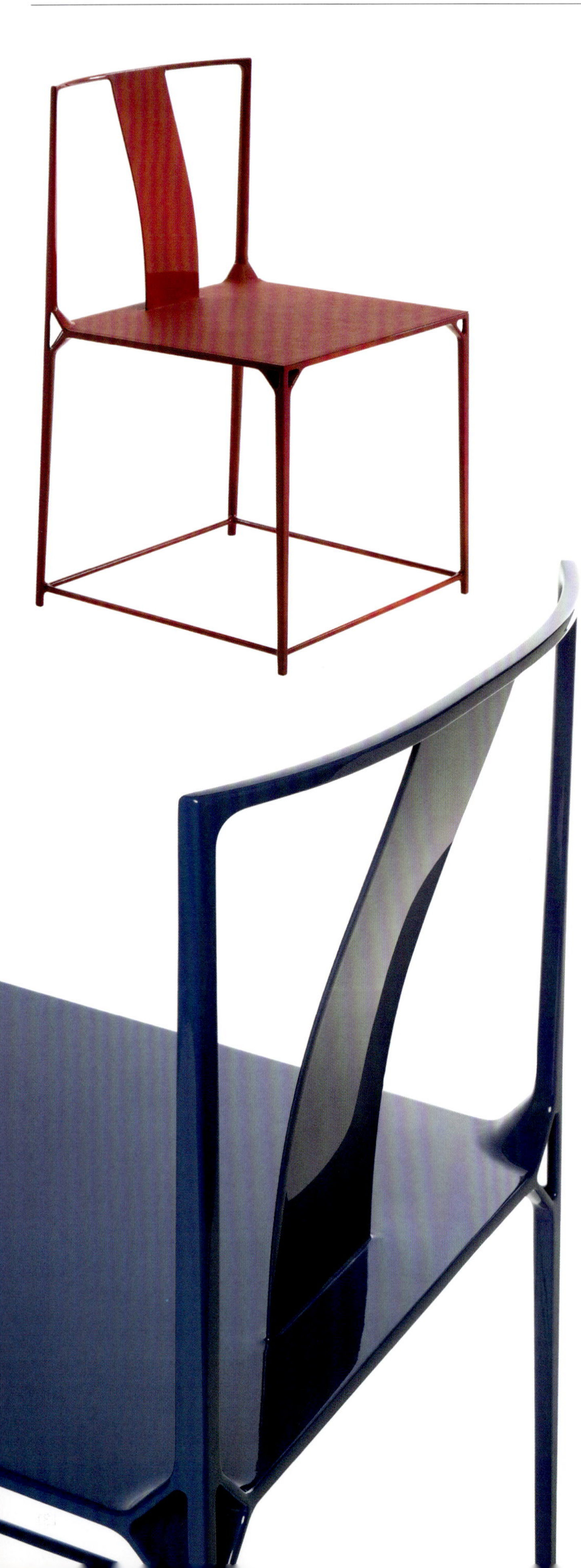

THE LUXURY OF MATERIALITY

Shang Xia is quite simply China's answer to Hermès, so much so that this extraordinary design-craft venture headed by Jiang Qiong Er is actually backed by the iconic French luxury brand. Indeed, its flagship store in Shanghai is next door to that of Hermès. It could be said to be a perfect Sino-French match because the two companies share the same dedication to preserving heritage and encouraging innovation through the active promotion and support of superlative craftsmanship and high-level design professionalism. Both are also united in placing an emphasis on the use of luxury materials and exquisite detailing. In terms of its furniture output, Shang Xia has two collections – one of exclusive, limited-edition pieces, and another that is more accessible yet still situated at the high end of the market. The three designs shown here come from the latter range and showcase the refined luxe-simplicity of the Shang Xia look, which is based on using different luxury materials in interesting and innovative ways. For instance, the Da Tian Di chair is made of high-tech carbon fibre, yet lacquered in the age-old Chinese tradition, while the elegant walnut rocking chaise incorporates a supple sling seat made of the most perfectly woven leather. By contrast, the Fuqi mini stools are made of *zitan* – a hardwood with a deep, almost purplish hue, which has been used in Chinese furniture production for centuries – and incorporate modern abstracted interpretations of traditional Chinese motifs, including a 'lucky' gourd.

←
DA TIAN DI WALNUT ROCKING CHAIR
by in-house design team for Shang Xia, 2010

↓
FUQI MINI STOOLS
by in-house design team for Shang Xia, 2017

A DESIGN-CRAFT ADVENTURE

As its founder, Jiang Qiong Er, explains, Shang Xia is all about 'a continuous melding of Eastern grace with French sophistication' and is intended to promote 'a sophisticated lifestyle that is exquisite yet simple'. By taking an almost art-based approach to the balancing of function and aesthetics, Jiang and her team of designers have produced some furniture pieces that are not only interesting in terms of their designs, which channel ancient Chinese forms, but also exquisite examples of masterful craftsmanship – with, for example, the Twilight folding screen, featuring light-filtering 'woven' panels of painstakingly pieced-together bamboo strips, and the Da Tian Di (Sky and Earth) tea table set made of *zitan*, a finely grained rosewood that has been used to make Chinese furniture for centuries, which has been beautifully constructed with seamless joinery. In a nod to traditional culture, the stools also feature age-old Chinese symbolism – the circle (heaven), the square (earth) and the circle within a square (the universe). The chairs are likewise adorned with traditional motifs, as well as with calligraphy, all of which are exquisitely carved into the dense wood with the utmost finesse.

↓
DA TIAN DI TEA TABLE SET
by in-house design team
for Shang Xia, 2012

→|
TWILIGHT BAMBOO PANELLED SCREEN
by in-house design team
for Shang Xia, 2016

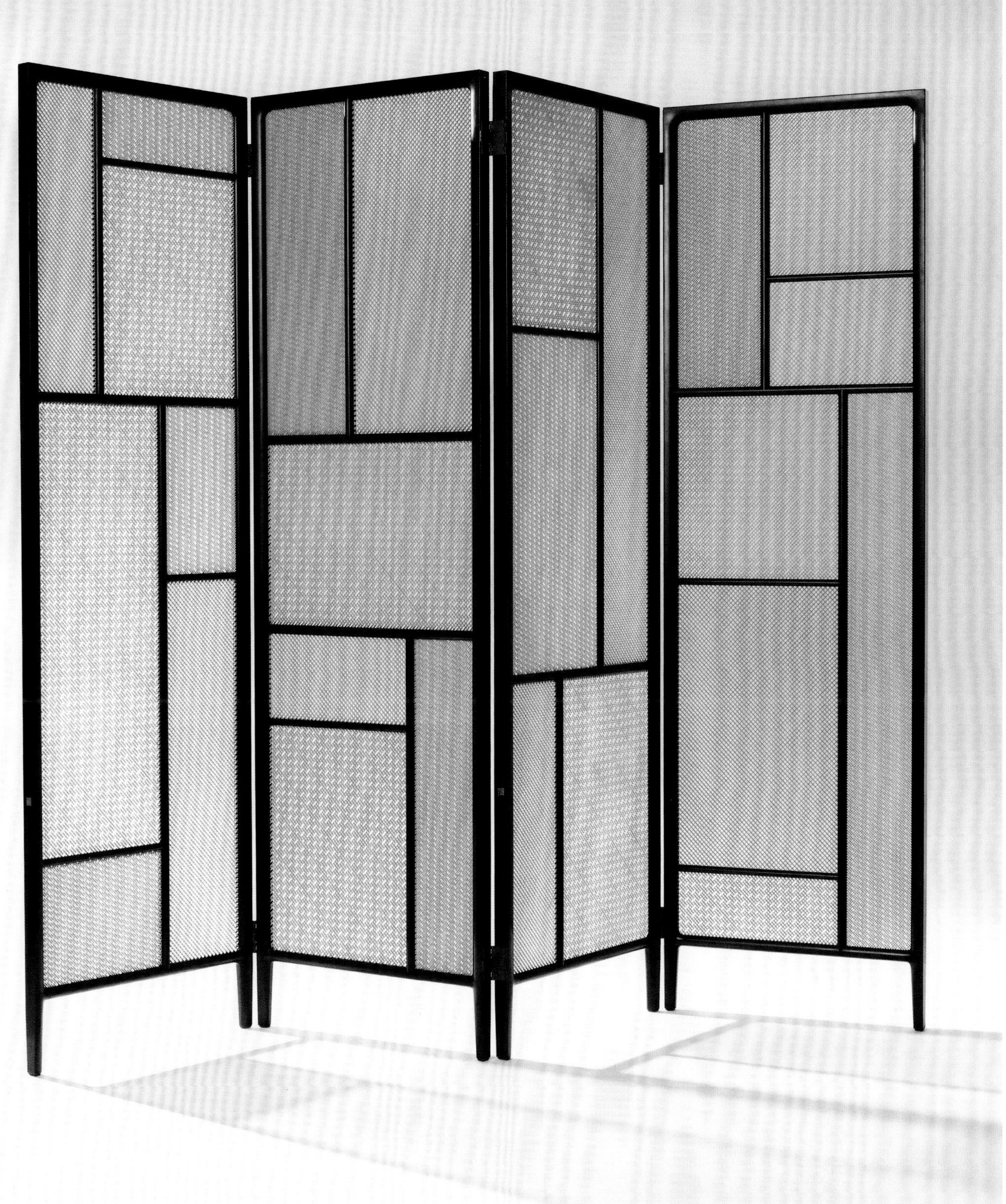

TOUCHING WOOD

Over the last decade, Jiang Qiong Er has been on an extraordinary design and craft adventure, which has resulted in the production of some remarkable furniture pieces that mark the creative pinnacle of contemporary Asian design. These superlative designs balance heritage with innovation, while reflecting a highly developed aesthetic sensibility that Jiang describes as, 'Pure yet sophisticated. Functional yet emotional. Oriental yet international. Poetic yet practical.' Shang Xia's two furniture collections are quite different, one features limited-edition, experimental pieces, which are the design equivalent of 'haute couture', while the other is more accessible and practical, yet still beautifully designed and crafted – a sort of very high-end 'ready-to-wear' collection. The designs shown here come from the latter range of furniture and are distinguished by the clever updating of traditional Ming forms, a sublime attention to harmonic proportions and exquisite detailing. These pieces, which are all designed by Shang Xia's talented in-house design team, possess an artisanal spirit and showcase a high level of skill in traditional joinery techniques, often used in new and unusual ways. Above all, this furniture collection – which includes a walnut table with a clever circular joint, a screen with leather-strapped canvas panels, and a beautifully proportioned luohan bed/couch – exemplifies Shang Xia's guiding mission of 'exquisite ordinariness'.

DA TIAN TIAN WALNUT BOOKSHELF
by in-house design team for Shang Xia, 2012

→
QIAN QUI WALNUT ROUND TABLE
by in-house design team for Shang Xia, 2016

↓
DA TIAN DI LUOHAN BED/COUCH
by in-house design team for Shang Xia, 2012

HIGH-TECH + AGE-OLD

In 2009 the designer Jiang Qiong Er established, in conjunction with the Hermès Group, the exclusive lifestyle brand Shang Xia (pronounced 'shang shah'), which means 'up/down'. The brand is focused on the creation of beautiful yet useful things, including furniture, accessories, homewares and fashion items, which preserve and revitalize traditional Chinese craftsmanship by expressing it through an exciting new language of contemporary design. One of Shang Xia's most impressive feats to date has been the execution of a series of furniture pieces designed by Gan Erke. These are made from a high-tech, lightweight yet strong carbon-fibre composite material that has been painstakingly coated with layers of lacquer and carefully polished to reveal a distinctive nodular pattern. This ancient lacquering technique, known as *bo luo* (rhinoceros skin) because of its distinctive patterning, was rediscovered by Gan from old treatises and took him many years to perfect. The spectacular Da Tian Di table and matching chair shown here, with their shimmering brown and gold lacquered surfaces, are quite simply masterpieces of contemporary design craft. They also represent an innovative and graceful evolution of Ming furniture forms achieved by combining traditional handicraft skills with state-of-the-art modern materials.

←
DA TIAN DI CHAIR
by Gan Erke for Shang Xia, 2017

↓
DA TIAN DI TABLE
by Gan Erke for Shang Xia, 2017

→|
Detail of the shimmering *bo luo*
lacquerwork on the Da Tian Di Table

SHAO FAN (YU HAN)

DECONSTRUCTING MING

Shao Fan is rightly considered to be an important founding father of New Chinese Design because his groundbreaking Chairs(?) series from the mid-1990s was a powerful creative catalyst for this still-emerging movement. Born into a renowned family of Beijing artists, Shao was taught painting by his parents, who, although university art professors, were tasked with producing propaganda art during the Cultural Revolution. Showing an early and prodigious gift for the arts, Shao went on to study at Beijing Arts and Crafts College (now Beijing University of Technology). There he received a traditional education that included learning various handicraft skills. This hands-on training stood him in good stead when later constructing his art-furniture pieces, and no doubt also inspired his lifelong appreciation of high-quality craftsmanship. After graduating in 1984, he began exploring three-dimensional art, while continuing to nurture his knowledge of Chinese culture by collecting antique furniture, woodcarvings and ceramics. In 1989 he began working as a full-time professional artist, and eventually set himself the challenge of creating a new series of art-furniture pieces that would symbolize China's cultural transformation. The resultant Chairs(?) series essentially spliced reproduction 'antique' Chinese chairs with modern abstracted forms reminiscent of Chinese characters, which were made of MDF. Sitting astride the fault line between art and design, these remarkable chair sculptures heralded a new Postmodern spirit within Chinese design. As Shao recalls, 'It was a very weird time in my life because no one had ever done anything like this before in China, and the initial reaction was "Wow", but in neither a good nor a bad way. But over the next ten years, this body of work inspired others and ultimately opened up thinking about Chinese design and its roots.' Its success also inspired Shao to create his thought-provoking and visually stunning Project No.1 chair of 2004, which explosively deconstructed an antique Ming chair to reveal its inner constructional secrets.

Work from 1995 no.1
by Shao Fan (self-production), 1995

Work from 1995 no.24
by Shao Fan (self-production), 1995

Project no.1 from 2004
by Shao Fan (self-production), 2004

DESIGN OR ART?

The well-known Chinese artist Shao Fan's maternal grandmother was descended from Chinese nobility, while his father's family was also high ranking. This meant that, very unusually for a child of his times, he grew up in a household furnished with Ming furniture and ceramics, and from a young age gained a rare appreciation of antiques. As a child growing up in the 1970s, he found it hard to reconcile the poor quality of contemporary Chinese clothing, crockery and buildings with the beautifully executed historic designs he saw when he visited the Imperial Palace. Even at 10 years old, he was acutely aware of this dichotomy, and to him it seemed that 'everything new was horrible and bad, and everything that was old was beautiful and good'. He started collecting old furniture, and always included furniture and architecture in his paintings because he wanted to convey a sense of human interaction. When he made his first art-furniture pieces in 1995, he did not care if they were considered art or design. For him it was the act of deconstruction that was key, for, as he explains, 'When you deconstruct a piece of Ming furniture, you see the secrets inside it. Most people experience just the outside of Ming furniture, but by deconstructing it you experience something else. When I opened it up for the first time, then all of a sudden it became my teacher. And with every mortise, I became more interested in design.' Although design had not been Shao's main concern in 1995 when he created his Chairs(?) series, by the early years of the twenty-first century his work was tending more towards usable design-art. His more recent furniture pieces, however, are more closely aligned to sculpture again, and are exquisitely executed explorations of the Ming aesthetic from a constructional, formal and psychological perspective. As Shao explains, 'all my work is about ideas, and my art informs my design, and my design informs my art'.

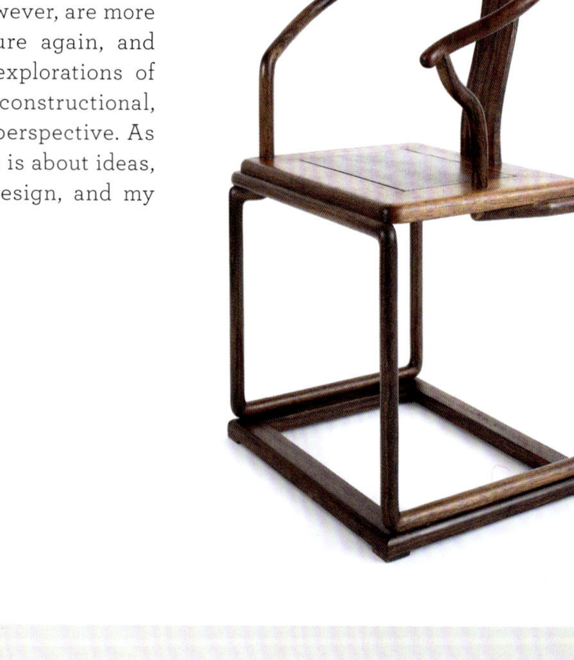

→|
Old tree chair
by Shao Fan (self-production), 2018

↑
Rose table
by Shao Fan (self-production),
2018 – its 'thorns' referencing the
origins of the rosewood it is made from

↗
Chair
by Shao Fan (self-production), 2013

→
Decorative stool
by Shao Fan (self-production), 2004

METALLIC MING

By the early 2000s the renowned Chinese artist Shao Fan, having already achieved international success with his Chairs(?) art-furniture series, turned his attention towards the creation of more functional furniture. Designed in 2000, his Round-backed Armchair made entirely of stainless steel exemplified this direction. It was launched as a limited edition of 70 pieces, each signed and dated. At this time the well-known gallerist Pearl Lam was representing Shao, and helped to generate international interest in his work by donating various pieces from his ever-growing Chairs(?) series to both London's Victoria & Albert Museum and New York City's Metropolitan Museum. The latter was given a pair of his sleek metal armchairs that channel historic Ming forms but in a very pared-down way. As the museum insightfully notes of them, they 'not only illuminate aesthetic connections across time and culture, but also demonstrate how China's past can both adapt and coexist with its rapidly changing and increasingly globalized present'. Wen Hao's later Fu Zi (Teacher's chair) similarly translates Ming forms into an eye-catching all-brass construction. A traditional Chinese armchair known as a *guanmaoyi* (Official's Hat chair) directly inspired this elegant high-backed rocking chair, but rather than making it from wood, Wen chose 'modern' tubular brass for the slender frame. He also used precisely shaped sections of sheet brass to create the subtly curved seat and back sections in order to provide a degree of comfort without the need for upholstery. The design is intended for use in study rooms, so it channels the so-called literati aesthetic, while its open-work form is supposed to 'symbolize the spirit of uncorrupted scholars and officials who have nothing but winds under their sleeves'. Wen's Yuezhu stool similarly transforms the historic form of an ancient drum stool into a thoroughly modern, metallic Neo-Ming piece.

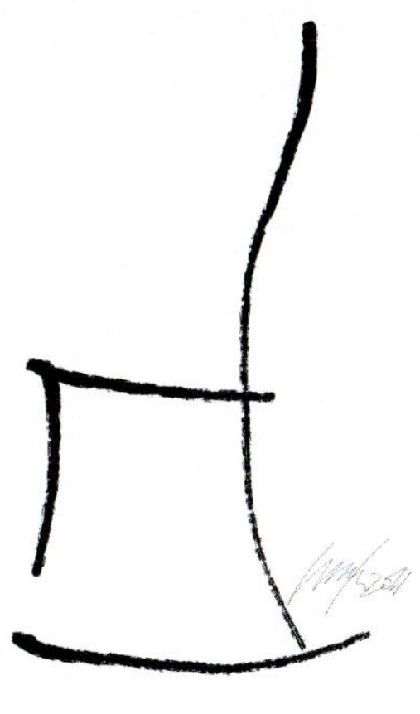

↑
Ink sketch of Fu (Teacher's chair) by Wen Hao, 2011

←
Yuezhu stool
by Wen Hao for Haostyle, 2013

↓
Fu zi (teacher's chair)
by Wen Hao for Haostyle, 2011

Round-backed armchair
by Shao Fan (self-production), 2000

SHEN BAOHONG/U⁺

MINIMALISM IS BLACK

While the majority of Shen Baohong's designs for U⁺ fall firmly within the Neo-Ming category, he also creates furniture pieces that have a more overt contemporary, minimalist aesthetic, even though they still at times directly reference historic forms. The ebonized folding chair shown here is a sophisticated interpretation of a traditional chair form that was popular during the Ming dynasty, while the low-slung armchair incorporates in its seating section the classic Taoist circle-in-a-square motif, symbolizing the harmonious joining of earth and heaven. In fact, Shen's use of monotone ebonized surfaces enhances his reductivist aesthetic, which lays bare the purity found in Ming forms. His sideboard and table, by contrast, are less directly inspired by the Ming style, but still retain a distinctive Chinese-ness thanks to his choice of materials and their easily recognizable Asian silhouettes. The copper drawer handles on the sideboard, for instance, echo a traditional form found time and again in historic Chinese furniture, yet Shen has skilfully updated and simplified the piece for life in the twenty-first century. More than anything, though, his work reflects his own self-effacing, scholarly disposition – it is, like him, thoughtful and quietly spoken.

↑
RU YI TABLE
by Shen Baohong for U⁺, 2017

←
MIAO JING SIDEBOARD
by Shen Baohong for U⁺, 2015

<u>Cheng qi armchair</u>
by Shen Baohong for U+, 2012

<u>T'ing yuan sidetable</u>
by Shen Baohong for U+, 2014

<u>Zuo wang zen chair</u>
by Shen Baohong for U+, 2013

←
Cheng xiang bookshelf
by Shen Baohong for U⁺, 2012

↗
Rong armchair
by Shen Baohong for U⁺, 2012

↗
Si ji sideboard
by Shen Baohong for U⁺, 2015

→
Cheng qi luohan bed/couch
by Shen Baohong for U⁺, 2017

THE AESTHETIC CALM OF SIMPLICITY

You could say that furniture-making runs in Shen Baohong's blood, for he is – very unusually for a Chinese furniture designer nowadays – a sixth-generation cabinet-maker. Certainly, the design and making skills that have been passed down within his family are immediately apparent in the furniture he creates for his company, U+, which is guided by the twin goals of harmony and moderation. Shen modestly credits his venture's success to his female business partner, who oversees its day-to-day operation, thereby allowing him to do what he does best – design furniture. The outcome is a range of refined Neo-Ming designs, which have a wonderful tactility thanks to the exquisite craftsmanship and attention to detail that go into their construction. All the U+ furniture shown here reflects Shen's ability to take historic Chinese furniture forms and give them a refreshing modern twist that is distinguished not only by perfect proportions and elegant lines, but also by a carefully considered simplification of form and a rare understanding of the functional requirements of contemporary life. It is Shen's masterful distilling of Ming forms down to their intrinsic essence that imbues his furniture with such a tangible sense of 'rightness' and aesthetic calm, and that ultimately makes his work so engaging.

THE SPIRIT OF MING

When surveying today's New Chinese Design scene, it is astonishing to witness the plethora of stylistic approaches that its designers are taking in their modern interpretations of ancient Song and Ming furniture. While some take a playful Neo-Postmodern approach, others are opting to pursue a Craft Revivalist route, or choosing more high-tech design-art expressions. What comes across clearly, however, is just how important China's historical furniture culture is to them, no matter how they choose to express it, and how much they want to build on its legacy. One of the designers who has best managed to revitalize the spirit of Ming within contemporary Chinese design is Shen Baohong. His superlative cabinet-making skills have enabled him to understand clearly the underlying constructional DNA, or design logic, of Ming furniture. This in turn has allowed him to create his own evolutions of it using a pared-down contemporary aesthetic. His designs have a simplified elemental quality that actually helps to enhance one's understanding of the superb functional rationality and aesthetic refinement of Ming furniture. But more than this, Shen's designs are beautifully designed and crafted, just like their historical antecedents.

↑
MING YUE CUPBOARD
by Shen Baohong for U⁺, 2014

←
KUAN ARMCHAIR
by Shen Baohong for U⁺, 2008
– based on the form of a Ming 'Official's Hat' chair, so named because it echoes the lines of the winged headwear worn by scholar-officials in the Song dynasty

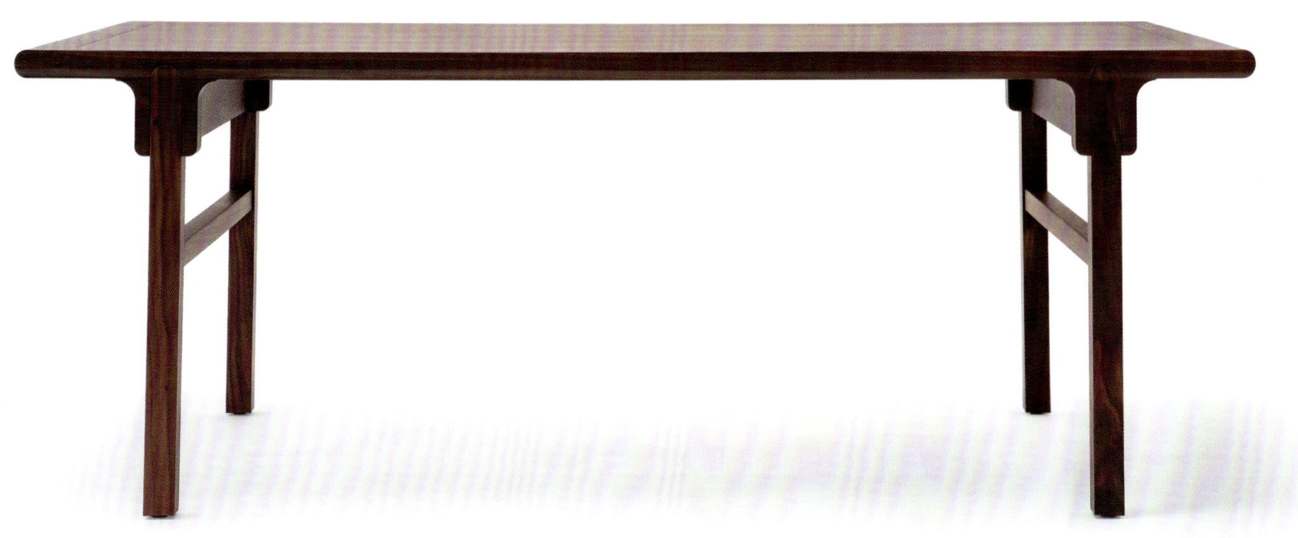

↑↑
RU YI ARMCHAIRS
by Shen Baohong for U⁺, 2016

↑
CHENG QI TABLE
by Shen Baohong for U⁺, 2014

<u>Mulan chair</u>
by in-house design team for
shiershiman, 2018

THOUGHTFUL TIMELESSNESS

The literal translation of shiershiman is '12 hours slow life', but the company is often referred to just as '12 Hours'. The name alludes to ancient Chinese timekeeping, which divided the day into 12 two-hour periods called *shi*. This somewhat curious name for a furniture company was chosen by its founders because, as they explain, 'Our ancestors believed that every hour of every day should be spent attentively and decently.' And that is exactly what they try to do themselves through their design of beautiful, high-quality, functionally considered furniture, which is imbued with a timeless elegance that comes from skilfully combining modern lifestyle considerations and contemporary aesthetics with an acknowledgement and promotion of China's great cultural traditions and crafts heritage. The Mulan chair and the clothes rack and dressing table shown here are all thoughtful modern interpretations of ancient Chinese furniture types, which have been cleverly updated for modern living and contemporary tastes. The mirror of the dressing table, for example, flips up and down so that it can be used while either seated or standing.

DRESSING TABLE
by in-house design team for
shiershiman, 2017

CLOTHES RACK
by in-house design team for
shiershiman, 2016

LIGHTING WITH A CHINESE TWIST

Truly creative innovation within the Chinese lighting sector is currently not as well developed as it is in, say, the design of seating or case furniture. There are, however, a few noteworthy exceptions. One of these is the lighting designed and manufactured by the new furniture brand shiershiman, which poetically evoke age-old Chinese forms. The Fishermen floor light, for example, was directly inspired by the suspended lanterns traditionally used by Chinese fishermen for night fishing, while the shape of its shade and base reference the woven conical hats worn by the fishermen. This simple yet sculpturally stylish design powerfully demonstrates how the contemplation of everyday objects can lead to the creative reimagining of both form and functionality. By contrast, shiershiman's Chinese Chivalry table lamp, with its distinctive tilting shade, looks to the imperial past for inspiration, in this case to *Qing Guanmao*, a type of woven rattan hat worn by officials during the Qing dynasty. Available in a host of different material options, this lamp is a masterful exercise in how to imbue a minimal design with emotionally engaging character.

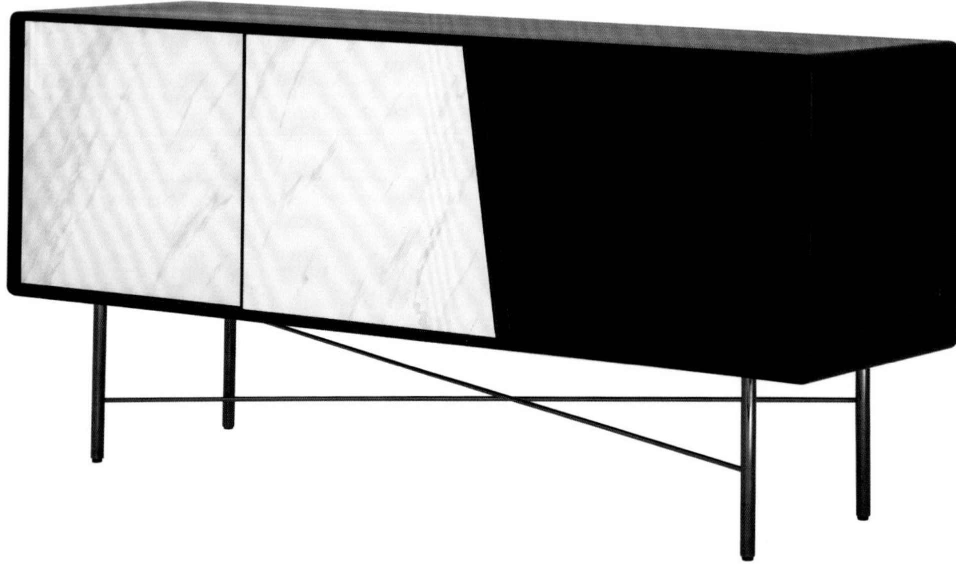

←
TWILIGHT CABINET
by in-house design team
for shiershiman, 2018

↓
TWILIGHT SIDEBOARD
by in-house design team
for shiershiman, 2018

LINE + PROPORTION

At a recent furniture exhibition in Shanghai, shiershiman's stand was conspicuous not only because of the high-quality furniture pieces on display, but also in terms of their presentation. Yet shiershiman is still very much in its infancy, having been founded in 2015. Nevertheless, its designs are on a par with those produced by much more established and famous design brands in Italy. Indeed, in many ways they are more aesthetically refined and visually interesting. To put it simply, shiershiman's output, by anyone's standards, is seriously impressive. Take, for example, its Twilight series, which comprises a sideboard, a large cabinet, a smaller side cabinet and a low-slung television cabinet, faced with white marble and executed to such exacting standards that their doors open and shut effortlessly. The company's great attention to detail can also be found in the design of the Pin sofa, with its practical leather and fabric cushion covers that can be mixed and matched and zipped on and off with ease. More than anything else, however, the refined lines and perfect proportions of these pieces set them apart and embody the new level of globally popular sophistication emerging in Chinese design.

PIN SOFA
by in-house design team
for shiershiman, 2017

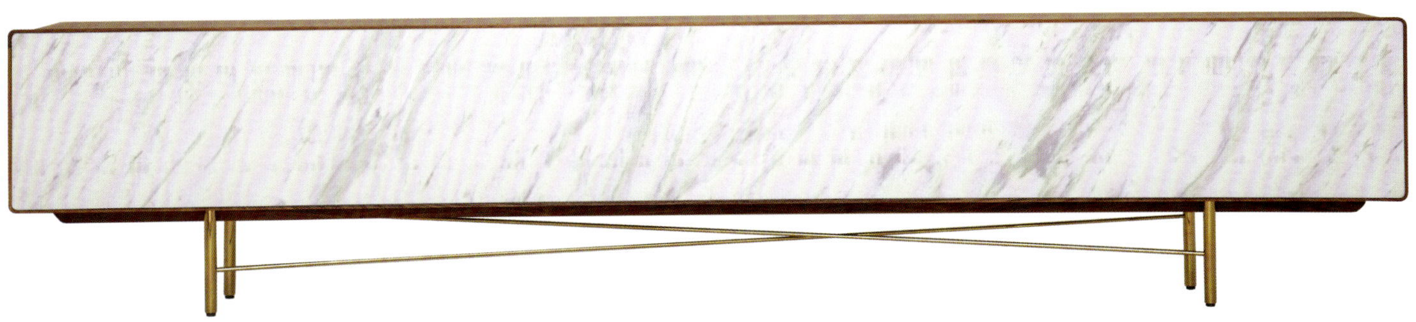

TWILIGHT LOW TELEVISION CABINET
by in-house design team
for shiershiman, 2018

JEFF DAYU SHI/DRAGONFLY DESIGN CENTER

THE BAMBOO MASTER

Award-winning Chinese designer Jeff Dayu Shi originally trained at the world-renowned Fashion Institute of Technology in New York, graduating in 1989. He then continued living in the Big Apple, where he worked as an in-house designer for the famous Harry Winston jewellery company. In 1996 he won the De Beers Diamond International Award, but that same year, wanting to explore new career opportunities as an artist and designer, he headed back East and established the Dragonfly Design Center – a pioneering design concept store in Taipei. His goal, as he explains, was 'to do something that comes from our Chinese roots, but which is innovative too, and that is representative of what has now become known as New Chinese Design.' His material of choice is bamboo, which he cherishes not only for its long and historic association with Chinese culture, but also because he believes it to be 'the material of the future', being an eminently renewable and therefore sustainable resource. Beyond these attributes, bamboo also possesses remarkable physical properties: it is both lightweight and strong, and when processed in certain ways can provide an inherent springy resilience, which is especially useful when it comes to designing seating. Over the years, Jeff has pioneered a number of low-tech yet highly innovative methods of working with bamboo, which involve various laminating methods. These have enabled him to create groundbreaking designs that take bamboo furniture to another level, both technically and aesthetically, as the designs shown here demonstrate so well.

↑↗
YI MAN FENG FOLDING MUSIC CHAIR
by Jeff Dayu Shi for Tong Pai Furniture,
2015 (and in folded position)

→
YI JUN ZI CHAIR
by Jeff Dayu Shi for Dragonfly Design
Center, 2010

→|
YI GE WU CHAIR
by Jeff Dayu Shi for Dragonfly Design
Center, 2018

↑
YI PING LIU YING SCREEN CHAIR
by Jeff Dayu Shi
for Dragonfly Design Center, 2017

→
YING GE MODULAR TEA CABINET
by Jeff Dayu Shi
for Dragonfly Design Center, 2017

EXPERIMENTING WITH BAMBOO

Jeff Dayu Shi is an acknowledged master of bamboo, utterly obsessed with his material of choice and endlessly experimenting to find innovative ways of incorporating it into his furniture designs. For example, he has devised a technique that uses thin slats of bamboo to create light-filtering panels, which he uses to great effect in his Screen chair and Flowing Shadow trolley-table. He also uses slatted bamboo for the construction of his Modular Tea Cabinet, which was inspired by an ancient imperial Chinese puzzle box in Beijing's Palace Museum. The small gaps between the cabinet's strips of bamboo crucially provide sufficient air circulation for the storage of fine teas. His Ba Shi reclining chaise, by contrast, exploits the natural springiness of flat bamboo strips. This 'zero gravity' design can be inverted in order alleviate backache, which Jeff himself suffers from. As his wife and business partner, Jennifer, notes, 'This has been one of the most technically challenging chairs that Jeff has ever created.' And no wonder, given the complexity of its all-bamboo construction. A New Chinese Design answer to Le Corbusier's LC4 chaise, this interesting design showcases the remarkable strength and resilience of bamboo, as well as Jeff's skills as a design innovator. He is also fascinated by historic Chinese bamboo craft culture, and through his research has discovered that bamboo-weaving techniques used in the past had different functional purposes. For example, one type of weave was used specifically for fishing baskets, while others were used for tea sieves or flower-arranging. His Ping Cha folding screen (shown overleaf) incorporates seven of these ancient weaving techniques, as well as a completely new technique he has developed himself, which involves stretching woven bamboo panels on to a frame instead of fixing them with glue.

Ping cha folding screen
by Jeff Dayu Shi for Dragonfly
Design Center, 2013

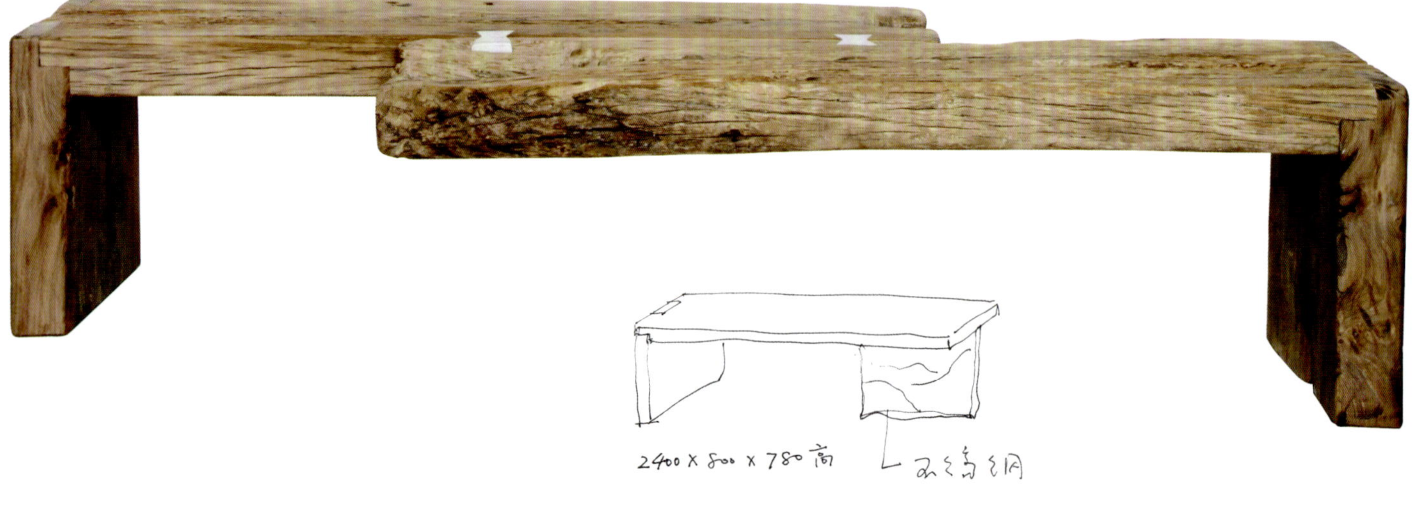

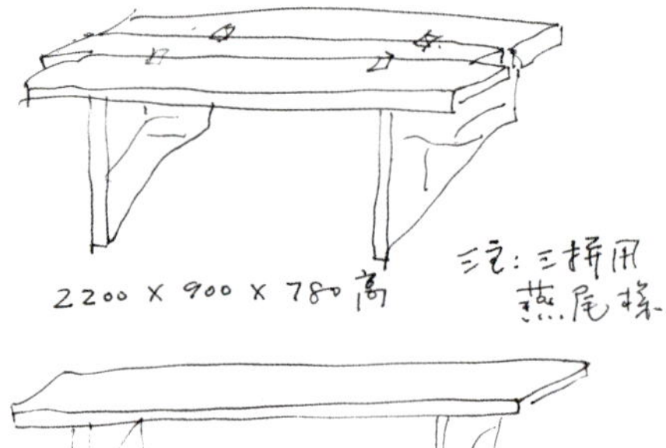

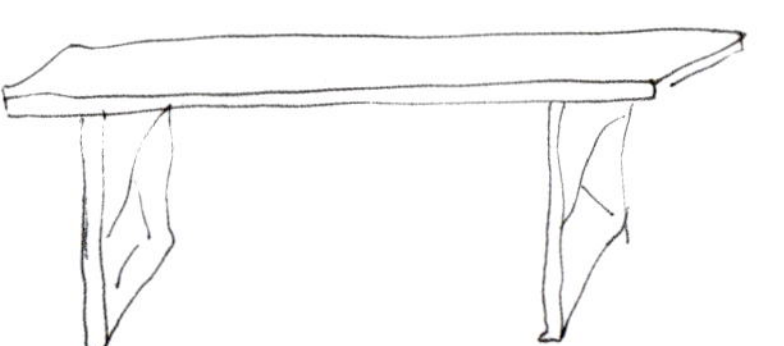

↑↑
RONG TABLE
by Song Tao for Self-Made Company, 2011

↑
ZHUI JI TABLE
by Song Tao for Self-Made Company, 2012

←
Design sketch showing three different steel
and elm slab tables, c. 2012

ANCIENT + MODERN

Song Tao is a legendary figure in Chinese design circles, having been the first director of Beijing Design Week, as well as an important pioneer of the New Chinese Style. He was also one of the very first Chinese designers to find success with experimental design-art furniture, and as such has been an inspiration to other Chinese designers following in his wake. Aside from his work as a designer and artist, he is also an influential gallerist, and has helped many young designers to establish themselves by showing their work. In 2002 he established his Self-Made Company in order to produce his own limited-edition designs, which are intended to revitalize 'Chinese spirits in furniture design', but in a very contemporary way. Song later established another venture called League in 2008, which involved getting Chinese artists to create artworks that incorporated wood and metal so as to rediscover and ultimately revitalize the Chinese tradition of working with these materials within the visual and applied arts. He subsequently created a series of furniture pieces that combined age-ravaged wood with gleaming metal to create a dynamic tension between old and new, ancient and modern. In many ways, these pieces, which include the bench and table shown here, can be seen as a commentary on contemporary Chinese society, which is constantly looking to the past, yet at the same time enthralled by the future. Song's later Modern Fossils series, which includes his iconic Gyrodes table, is likewise inspired by China's dynamic and changeable environment, and seeks to question the concept of time and the significance of history. The acrylic-encased 'denaturalized' wooden tabletop is a metaphor for modern urban society, and the bronze bamboo elements represent youthful vitality growing out of the past, which is symbolized by the use of ancient 'fossilized' wood.

FOSSILS

Song Tao, alongside his friend and erstwhile colleague Shao Fan, is one of the great fathers of Chinese art furniture. He initially studied graphic design and drawing at the National University of Art and Design in Beijing, then took a master's degree in the plastic arts at Sorbonne University in Paris, where he was introduced to the concept of art furniture. He returned to China after graduating in 1993, and established the TAO gallery in Shanghai the following year. Over time, this venture became very influential and exhibited the work of many leading Chinese artists and designers. Song subsequently established his own design studio, which specializes in furniture, interiors and exhibitions. His early furniture tended to feature slabs of ancient wood pieced together using polished steel elements, thereby mixing the old with the new. Indeed, throughout his career as a designer, Song's work has blended ancient Chinese philosophy with a Western contemporary attitude, and his furniture cleverly juxtaposes Oriental craft culture against Occidental minimalism. This has led him to develop a technique of 'fossilizing' wood in acrylic, thereby (as he says) 'denaturizing' it. He uses these slabs of wood suspended in synthetic polymer to create limited-edition design-art furniture, such as the table shown here, the top of which looks as though it is encased in amber, while being precariously balanced on three bamboo-like metal struts. As he notes, 'Bronze bamboo represents the spirit of strong vitality and never-ending youth, while old wood is a natural material. [My] amber fossils symbolize the solidification of the time.'

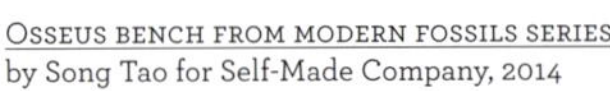

OSSEUS BENCH FROM MODERN FOSSILS SERIES
by Song Tao for Self-Made Company, 2014

SONG TAO + WU ZUOGUANG

TRANSLUCENCE + OPACITY

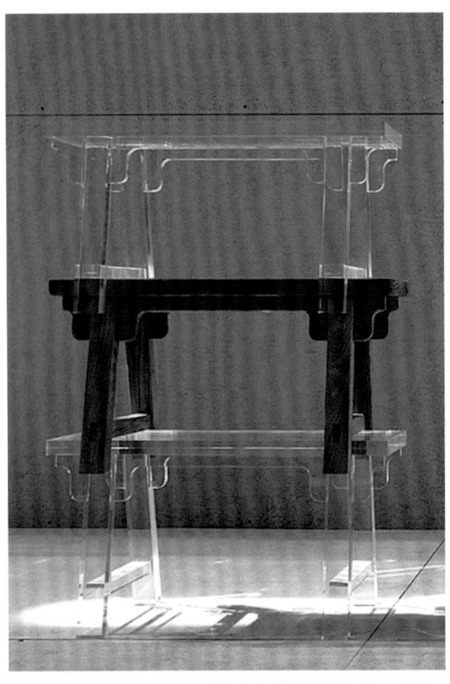

In 2011 Song Tao created a visually dynamic art-furniture series that contrasted transparent acrylic with old timbers. Some of these designs directly reference traditional Chinese furniture forms, such as the bench stools that stack to form shelves, or the armchairs that are inspired by Ming forms. However, other pieces in the series, such as the bench and table, are much less obvious in their referencing of historic typologies, and therefore have a stronger contemporary aesthetic, which is nevertheless very Chinese in spirit. While these pieces have an almost ethereal visual lightness and a distinct poetic quality, they also possess a strong nostalgic and emotional resonance thanks to Song's incorporation of ancient slabs of wood. In fact, the fusion of old materials (wood) with new ones (acrylic) reflects the Taoist belief that harmony is achieved when opposites are held in perfect balance. Likewise, the contrasting of translucency and opacity – in other words, light and dark – also reflects the Taoist concept of yin and yang. Song's work reflects not only his interest in the intrinsic dialogue between form, function and materials, but also his skill in balancing *feng shui* principles with a Western aesthetic sensibility when working in the context of interior design.

←
RONG STOOLS
by Song Tao
for Self-Made Company, 2011

↓
TAO TABLE
by Song Tao
for Self-Made Company, 2011

UNDULATING CHINESE LINES

Wu Zuoguang is highly regarded among his peers within the Chinese furniture industry for being not only Professor of Industrial Design at Zhejiang Sci-Tech University, but also the founder of the SUREECO® Furniture company. Like many of his compatriots he believes that the time is ripe for a renaissance within Chinese furniture design, for as he notes, 'We should have our own contemporary furniture design, which is not imported from the West, nor a copy of the designs of our ancestors. Many aspects of our traditional culture such as traditional Huizhou architecture and Ming and Qing furniture don't belong to the present, for technology, the environment and people's needs have all changed completely.' But for Wu, this does not mean that designers should not accept 'the gifts of our ancestors' in order to obtain inspiration for the creation of new era products. In fact, he has held this belief since he first began designing furniture back in 2003, which is distinguished by the use of undulating, almost calligraphic, lines that are very Chinese in spirit. Like many other Chinese designers, Wu believes in the conception of furniture within larger compositions. It is this holistic understanding of design as it relates to overall lifestyle that is key to understanding what is so different and interesting about the emerging New Chinese design movement. These are designs intended to create an atmosphere, to provoke a sense of spirit.

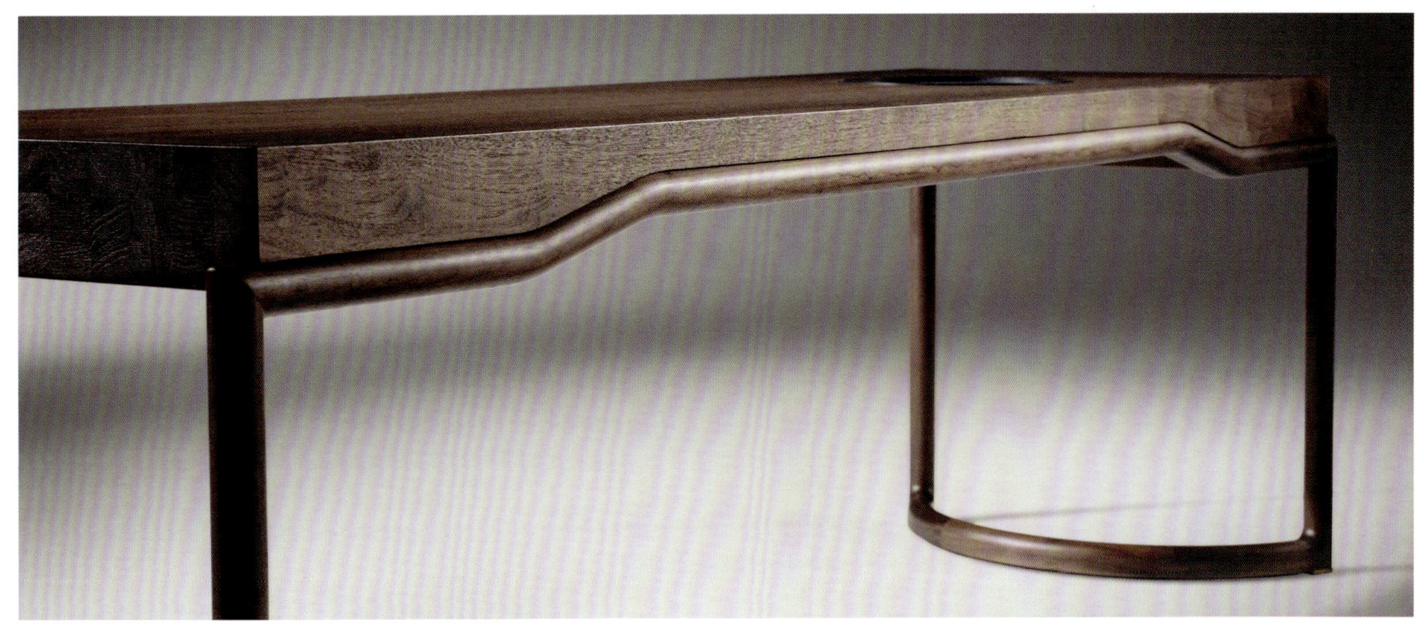

↑
UTILITY DINING TABLE
by Neri&Hu
for Stellar Works, 2018

↖
UTILITY CHAIR
by Neri&Hu
for Stellar Works, 2018

↙
UTILITY TWO-SEATER SOFA
by Neri&Hu
for Stellar Works, 2018

LOOKING INWARDS,
LOOKING OUTWARDS

Founded in 2012, Stellar Works is a Franco-Japanese venture based in Shanghai. Its founder, Yuichiro Hori, explains that the intention behind this China-based brand was 'to bring ideas together: East and West, heritage and modernity, craft and industry – bringing the best of the past into the light of the present'. Like a number of other recently established China-based furniture brands, Stellar Works manufactures work by a roster of international designers. It has also reissued 'classic' mid-century designs by the likes of Vilhelm Wohlert and Jens Risom. The company's creative direction is, however, very Chinese in its focus, being overseen by Neri&Hu, an interdisciplinary architectural design practice based in Shanghai and London and led by the architects Lyndon Neri and Rossana Hu. While both are Chinese, they grew up in the Philippines and Taiwan region respectively, and met in America while studying at UC Berkeley. Both share the desire to change the Western perception of Chinese design and seek a meaningful Chinese identity within their own work. Take, for example, their Utility collection for Stellar Works, which nostalgically references the Maoist-influenced '30 Years' style. These elegant and versatile pieces have an engaging retro-industrial aesthetic, yet still accord with Stellar Work's goal of 'Asian sensibility, timeless craft'.

<u>Utility round wall mirror</u>
by Neri&Hu
for Stellar Works, 2018

THE SCANDINAVIAN CONNECTION

The word *huaren* refers to ethnic Chinese, while the term *huayì* refers to people of Chinese descent who live outside China, all members of the vast Chinese diaspora. In Singapore, for example, 76 per cent of the population identified themselves in 2015 as either *huaren* or *huayì*. Given this, we felt that a survey on contemporary Chinese furniture design would not be complete without including some Singaporean Chinese designers. Among these is Gabriel Tan, who studied at the National University of Singapore, then briefly at the École cantonale d'art in Lausanne. He subsequently interned at Lunar Design in San Francisco, one of the most prestigious multidisciplinary design agencies in the world. On returning to Singapore, Tan founded the Outofstock design collective with three other young designers: Wendy Chua from Singapore, Gustavo Maggio from Argentina and Sebastián Alberdi from Spain. The name of the collective alludes to the fact that they originally met in Stockholm, while working at the Electrolux Design Lab. The hugely talented Tan is one of a handful of Chinese designers whose work is being manufactured by well-known design-led manufacturers overseas, namely Blå Station (Sweden), Design Within Reach (USA) and Ariake (Japan). His diminutive Stove chair – inspired by the form of a Shaker cooking stove, as well as the wall pegs used for hanging up chairs in Shaker homes – is a tour de force of East-meets-West fusion design, its Scandinavian simplicity perfectly twinned with an oriental aesthetic refinement. It is rare to find a young designer with such a deep understanding of form and function, and Tan is undoubtedly a rising Asian design star worth watching.

↤ & ↘↘
STOVE CHAIR
by Gabriel Tan
for Blå Station, 2018

↓
SKY LADDER BOOKCASE
by Gabriel Tan
for Ariake, 2017

↙↙
RIKYU MEDIA CONSOLE
by Gabriel Tan
for Ariake, 2017

TAN ZHIPENG + LUO DAI-SHI/MÁN-MÁN DESIGN

FLUID ORGANICISM

Tan Zhipeng and Luo Dai-Shi established Mán-mán Design in 2015 and are already seen as being in the vanguard of contemporary Chinese design art, having exhibited annually at Design Miami/Basel since their studio's founding. In 2017 the duo also received funding from China National Arts as part of its Young Art Talents award, testifying to the high regard in which these young artists are already held. Their materials of choice are brass and copper, which have been used extensively in China for millennia, yet they sculpt them into beautiful abstract forms that are derived from the natural world. Tan's specialism is lost-wax casting, while

Luo has dedicated herself to the colouring and patination of these metals. Together, they enjoy exploring metals from their physical and chemical perspectives in order to express through their designs the materials' intrinsic properties. Their creations are very much a collaborative effort, with Tan taking the lead in their design conception, and Luo being more involved in their execution. They can be seen as experimental explorations of form, function and material. Their Lotus series includes a console table, stool, high side table and low two-tiered coffee table, each of which is made of polished cast brass as a limited-edition of 12 pieces.

→
Lotus console table
by Tan Zhipeng for Mán-Mán
Design (self-production), 2016

↘
Lotus coffee table
by Tan Zhipeng for Mán-Mán
Design (self-production), 2017

←
LOTUS HIGH SIDE TABLE
by Tan Zhipeng for
Mán-Mán Design (self-
production), 2015

↙
LOTUS STOOL
by Tan Zhipeng for
Mán-Mán Design (self-
production), 2015

METALLIC POETRY

Mán-Mán Design's first critical success came with its 33 Step chairs and stools from the Bones series (2015–16), which took as its direct inspiration spinal columns and other human bones. Since then, the company's founders, Tan Zhipeng and Luo Dai-Shi, have moved on to creating limited-edition design-art furniture pieces that are much more organically abstract and consequently have a far greater sculptural boldness. Tan's Shengji series, made of burnished and matt-finished cast brass, for example, includes designs that are based formally on the structure of lotus roots and lotus-pad formations, which give the designs a dynamic sense of organic growth. By contrast, his stainless-steel Shengji-Sofa (shown overleaf) – which weighs a whopping 140 kg (300 lb) – has a much more 'blobular' aspect, its mirror-finished surfaces accentuating the different material properties of this hard, cold and highly reflective alloy. It is, however, the curious Walking Coffee Table, made of bronze, that is the weirdest of Tan's designs, with its lotus pad-inspired top supported on a mass of root-like legs that look as though they might at any minute scuttle off like some out-of-this-world mutant creature.

↓
Walking coffee table
by Tan Zhipeng
for Mán-Mán Design, 2017

↦ & ↘↘
Shengji-star chair (and detail)
by Tan Zhipeng
for Mán-Mán Design, 2017

↘
Shengji side table
by Tan Zhipeng
for Mán-Mán Design, 2017

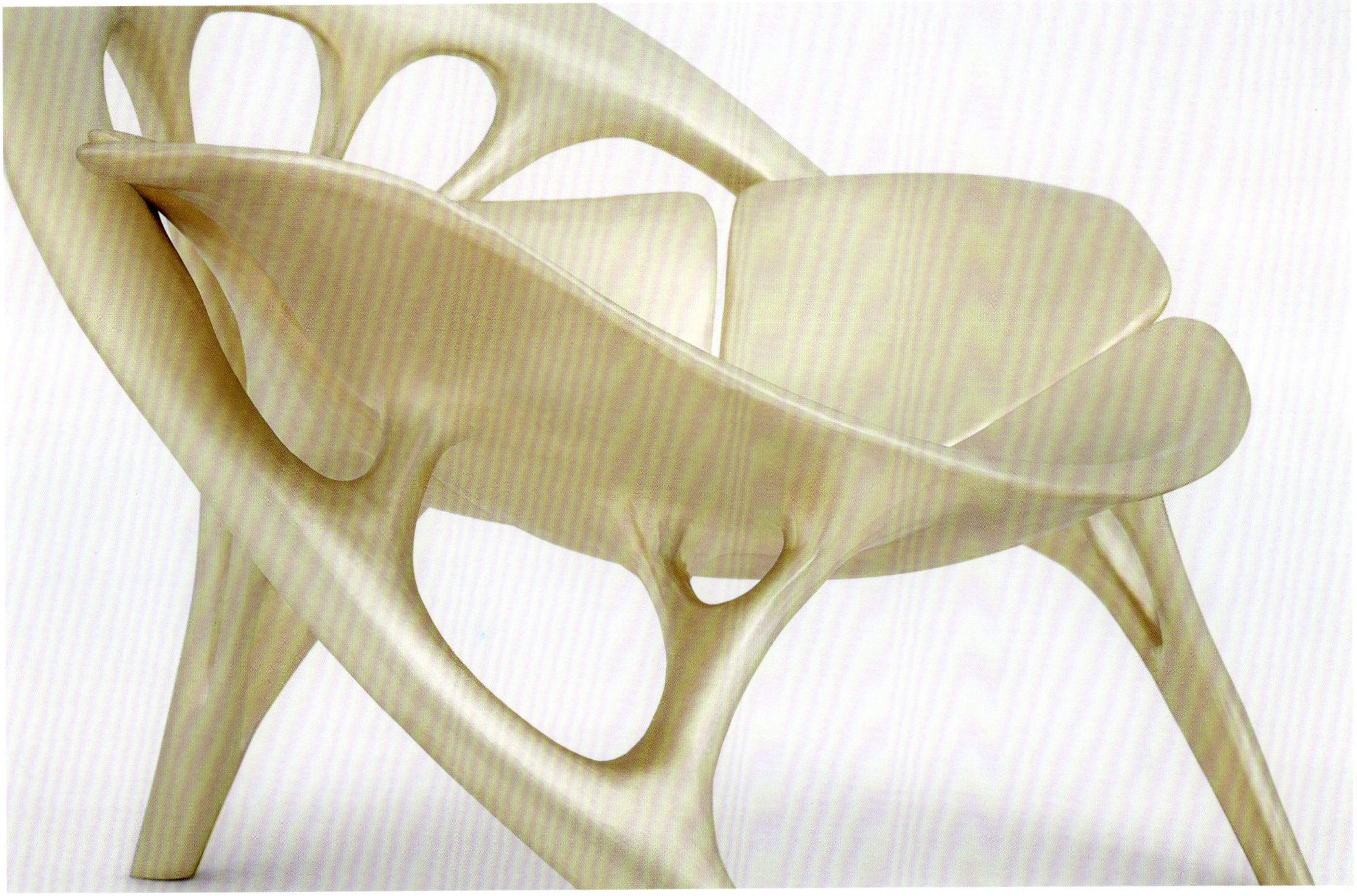

SHENGJI-SOFA
by Tan Zhipeng
for Mán-Mán Design, 2017

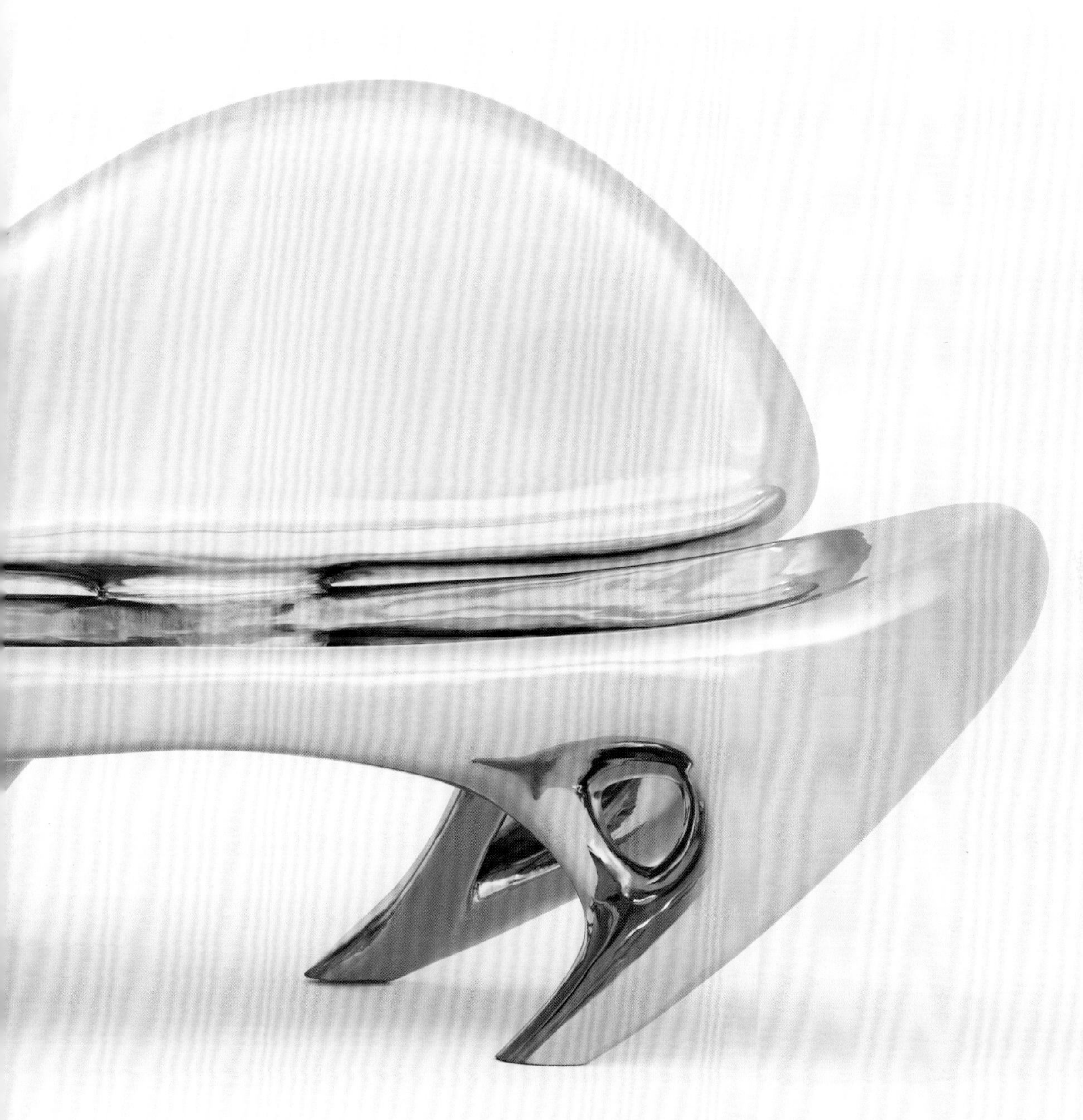

PURE DESK
by Mario Tsai
for Zaozuo, 2017

BASKET SIDE TABLES
by Mario Tsai
for Mario Tsai Studio, 2015

CUDDLE CHAIR
by Mario Tsai
for Lost&Found, 2018

Detail of CUDDLE CHAIR

SINO-MINIMALISM

Mario Tsai is a talented young Chinese designer who founded his own design studio in Hangzhou in 2014. Since then, he has forged a name for himself with his simple yet chic minimalist furniture, such as his steel and plywood Basket side tables, which made their debut in 2015. These eye-catching and lightweight designs, which are cleverly composed of a shelf-like frame on to which removable tray-like tabletops are fitted, can be carried in one hand. As Tsai observes, although the designs look as though they are defying gravity and will topple at any moment, 'they are actually very stable'. More recently, he has been working with Lost&Found on the new Core collection, which is aimed at the contract market, but is still intended to perpetuate the brand's ethos of domesticated simplicity. Tsai's retro-inspired Cuddle chair, for example, echoes the arching arms seen in Lost&Found's earlier Tianjin Iron Pipe Chair of 2008, but, as its creator explains, 'Compared with the earlier design, this new one is aimed at improving the sense of security, and using enclosed arms just helped solve this problem in a clever way.' Tsai's work is fundamentally all about creating elegant yet simple furnishing solutions with a sustainable approach to design and manufacturing. The resulting designs have a soft yet pure minimalist aesthetic that is predicated on a minimal use of materials and processes in their construction.

←
YUN (CLOUD DRAGON) CHAIR
by Wen Hao
for Haostyle, 2011

↓
DETAIL OF YUN CHAIR
by Wen Hao
for Haostyle, 2011

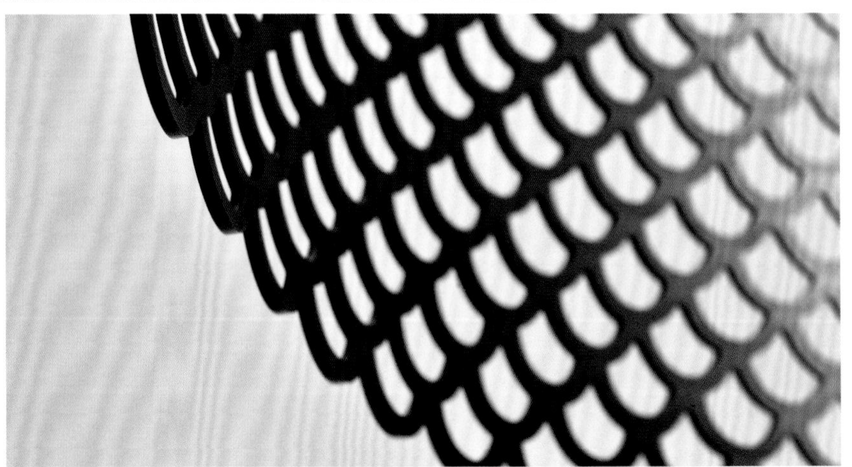

BEYOND THE CLASSICAL

In China there is a well-established tradition for university professors who teach design to work concurrently as professional interior or furniture designers. Those who do often go on to establish their own successful design-led brands, and it is these individuals who are held in the highest esteem. Indeed, in China the idea of learning from a master is a culturally entrenched concept. Renowned as an artist, scholar and curator, Wen Hao, who is dean of the Institute of Furniture at the Guangzhou Academy of Fine Arts, is widely regarded as a veritable guru of contemporary furniture design. Alongside Shao Fan and Song Tao, Wen is considered one of the 'first generation' of New Chinese Design, and many of his students have gone on to become star designers of the

so-called second and third generations. One of the reasons Wen is so revered is that he established the very first contemporary furniture gallery in China in 1996, importing cutting-edge designs from abroad. He went on to found Haostyle in 2006, with his wife acting as its business manager. This fledgling brand quickly became famous in China thanks to its very expensive and distinctive all-brass Neo-Ming furniture, which was based on Wen's desire to modernize and re-energize Chinese tradition by fusing advanced production technology with artisanal craftsmanship. His best-known design is the Yun (Cloud Dragon) chair, with its dragon-patterned leather seat, which pushes the classical canon of Chinese forms into a thoroughly contemporary *huaren* aesthetic.

WU WEI/THRUDESIGN

ENLIGHTENED DESIGN AND MANUFACTURING

An industrial designer by training, Wu Wei worked at the highest level in that sector, being the design director of Founder Tech for over ten years. During this time, however, he became increasingly concerned about the ever-shortening life cycle of consumer products. Worried that 'more and more products were being turned into garbage in less than a year', he began designing solid wood furniture as a sort of antidote, the objective being to create something with inherent longevity. He subsequently founded his own small design consultancy in 2011 with the idea of working on just one industrial design project per year, and devoting the rest of his time to designing furniture, which he hoped would be produced by an existing manufacturer. After a difficult first year of rejections, he eventually found a manufacturer to work with and began producing his beautifully crafted furniture pieces, which reference Ming forms using a contemporary minimalist language of design. At the same time, he also opened an allied workshop to teach people basic Western woodworking techniques. The aim was to provide them with hands-on experience that would help them to 'reconnect with things' in an increasingly atomized society. Vis-à-vis his own furniture designs, he wanted 'to do something with a Chinese feel, but that wasn't superficial', so he took it upon himself to learn as much as possible about traditional Chinese furniture-making techniques. As a devout Buddhist, it was also important for him to take a holistic and ethical approach to both design and making. One of the ways he does this is by creating furniture that has an innate simplicity and that uses only FSC-accredited woods – maple, walnut and cherry. In fact, he completely rejects the use of rarer hardwoods, observing, 'we are not living in Ming times'.

←

YOU RONG SIDEBOARD
by Wu Wei and design team
for Thrudesign, 2015

↑

QIN CHAIR
by Xue Fei and design team
for Thrudesign, 2018

↗

LING KONG SIDE TABLE
AND MING ARMCHAIR
by Wu Wei and design team
for Thrudesign, 2012

→

LONG BENCH TABLE
by Xue Fei and design team
for Thrudesign, 2013

SIMPLICITY = SPIRITUALITY

Wu Wei is aware that many people nowadays have become disconnected from the material origins of the things they use, so his hands-on carpentry workshop is a way of attempting to get them reconnected. For instance, when a class of children come in for the day, he always explains the life cycle of a tree because he wants to convey the message that wood is from nature and is therefore a precious resource. He also realizes that it is far too easy for an ancient forest to be destroyed for the sake of a dining suite, so he takes care to ensure that any woods he uses for his own furniture are from verifiably sustainable sources. In fact, his whole approach to design is holistic and mindful. He understands, for example, that touch is important for both physical and psychological connections, so he makes sure that his furniture has beautifully smooth surfaces, with rounded corners to prevent injury to children or the elderly. As a Buddhist, meditation is also an important feature of Wu's life, and many of his seating designs facilitate a sitting posture to enhance the flow of *chi* (energy). He has also created a suite of furniture specifically for meditating. This features a beautifully painted screen, a slightly raised platform and a Song dynasty-inspired stool, which functions as an arm prop when lying in a semi-recumbent position. Achieving a great sense of transcendental spirituality through its refined simplicity, this is a truly remarkable arrangement of furniture, but, as Wu says, 'design should not be obvious, but just part of life'.

←
TING ZHONG STOOL/ARM PROP
by Xue Fei and design team
for Thrudesign, 2018

↗
TING ZHONG SCREEN, TING ZHONG
RAISED PLATFORM WITH TING ZHONG
STOOL AND LING KONG SIDE TABLE
by Wu Wei and design team
for Thrudesign, 2018

→|
WU XIANG LOW-BACKED MEDITATION
SEAT WITH WU XIANG CABINET
by Wu Wei and design team
for Thrudesign, 2017

by Xiao Tianyu
(self-production), 2010

SEARCHING FOR HARMONY

Xiao Tianyu studied design at the China Central Academy of Fine Arts in Beijing, graduating in 2010. For his final graduation project, he designed a series of chairs that combined upholstered, boulder-like bases with wooden backs based on simplified traditional Chinese furniture forms. Entitled 'Harmony', this eye-catching furniture group helped to establish Xiao as one of the most innovative young designers emerging from the New Chinese Design movement in Beijing at the time. Indeed, this student work was widely publicized not only in China, but also abroad. By channelling local cultural references in a highly refreshing way, Xiao sought with this furniture collection to create designs that had both an elegant simplicity and a contemporary sculptural aesthetic that was unequivocally Chinese in flavour. The critical success of the Harmony series encouraged Xiao to use it as a thematic blueprint for his later furniture collections, which must be seen as refined evolutions of this early yet important student work.

POETIC LANDSCAPES

Having found early success as a graduate with his eye-catching Harmony series of 2010, which married 'Western' padded pouf forms with 'Eastern' wooden back rails, Xiao Tianyu decided to continue exploring this hybrid East-meets-West theme in his later Growing Tree series. Comprising a sofa, chair, stools and a table, this limited-edition collection of eight units per design is one of the most poetic expressions of New Chinese Design to date. The back rails are executed from dark-hued rosewood, a material that is still highly prized in China thanks to its historic associations with imperial luxury, despite its use being seen in some quarters as ecologically controversial. Certainly, using this rare hardwood in the creation of long-lived and beautifully executed design-art pieces is more justifiable than if it were used to make mass-produced, run-of-the-mill furniture. The fact that Xiao's Growing Tree series makes direct reference to the origin of the material used to make it is itself a poetic statement, and invites reflection on the deeply intertwined yet complex relationship between Chinese culture and the natural world.

↓
GROWING TREE SOFA AND STOOLS
by Xiao Tianyu
(self-production), 2016

→
GROWING TREE TABLE
by Xiao Tianyu
(self-production), 2016

↘
GROWING TREE CHAIR
by Xiao Tianyu
(self-production), 2016

←
Inheritance low armchair
by Xiao Tianyu
(self-production), 2011

↓
Inheritance sofa
by Xiao Tianyu
(self-production), 2011

THE IMPERIAL AESTHETIC

Like other designers working in China today, Xiao Tianyu draws inspiration from the rich culture of the Ming dynasty in order to create furniture that is authentically Chinese in spirit while also being thoroughly modern and outward-looking. His Inheritance armchair and sofa are low-slung, super-stylish interpretations of Ming furniture forms, while his Bron chair takes the back-rail form of a traditional Ming 'Official's Hat' chair and sinks it into a circular, leather-covered pouf to dramatic sculptural effect. By contrast, his stunning brass and ebony Cloud table and chair glitteringly channel a more overtly imperial aesthetic, but in a Neo-Postmodernist way. In lesser hands this look can seem rather nouveau riche and gauche, but Xiao's interpretation of this style is pitch perfect. To this extent, his work, which is also inspired by his interest in traditional arts and crafts techniques, must be seen as twenty-first-century explorations of historic national culture. Xiao's goal is to produce designs that possess a 'unified elegant simplicity' and that pull the best of the past into the present.

↓
<u>BRON CHAIR</u>
by Xiao Tianyu
(self-production), 2016

↓↓
<u>CLOUD TABLE AND CHAIR</u>
by Xiao Tianyu
(self-production), 2015

XU MING + VIRGINE MORIETTE/STUDIO MVW

ANCIENT + MODERN,
EAST + WEST

In the vanguard of contemporary Chinese design, Xu Ming and Virgine Moriette of Studio MVW playfully mix ancient Chinese forms and motifs with a more modern Western sensibility in order to create furniture pieces that have an undeniably Sino-French élan. For instance, the title and form of their limited-edition Shuidi bookshelves (overleaf) take their inspiration from a drop of water – water being perceived as the greatest 'yin' character (negative, dark and feminine) among the five elements. In another nod to Chinese symbolism – this time to the circle, which means perfection, oneness, unity or harmony – their Yue armchair (overleaf) is made up of a series of looping brass-anodized tubular-steel elements. Their Cotton armchair, by contrast, takes a traditional Ming chair form and innovatively updates it by using matt-finished, ebony-stained oak and white leather. It is, however, the U Collection that perhaps represents the duo's most interesting series of furniture designs to date. Inspired by the traditional Chinese craft of paper-cutting known as *jianzhi*, the range is based on the idea of a single U-shaped form that can be 'cut out' to create different functional applications as well as aesthetic variations. The U Collection incorporates 12 sculptural chairs, plus various shelving units, benches and dining tables. Fusing Chinese spirit with twenty-first-century engineering-led production techniques, this remarkable furniture range constitutes a refreshingly innovative approach to contemporary Chinese design.

U COLLECTION
by Studio MVW
for He Yi, 2011

→|
COTTON ARMCHAIR
by Studio MVW
(self-production), 2009

↳
YUE ARMCHAIR
by Studio MVW
(self-production), 2017

↳|
SHUIDI BOOKSHELVES
by Studio MVW
(self-production), 2009

NEW CHINESE BRONZES

Inspired by the bronzes of ancient China, Xu Ming and Virgine Moriette of Studio MVW have created two truly remarkable bronze furniture collections that are not only stylishly elegant, but also have a strong sculptural presence. Known as the Xiangsheng I and Xiangsheng II series, these limited-edition design-art pieces deliberately play on the core Chinese philosophy that the balancing of opposites is the way to achieve harmony, in this case by setting solids against voids, and 'aged' oxidized surfaces (in deep brown and verdigris hues) against newer-looking brushed ones. But more than this, the collection can also be seen as a fusion of Eastern and Western design ideals, for as the couple explain, 'In the West, a solid object is seen in terms of materials and form and admired for that. In the East, the concept of emptiness is meaningful, and can be traced back to the Taoist philosophy to represent the spirit void of thought, a quiet, patient place from which the subliminal can flow.'

<u>Xiangsheng I side table #1,</u>
<u>Xiangsheng I side table #2 and</u>
<u>Xiangsheng I side table #3</u>
by Studio MVW (self-production), 2015

Xiangsheng II modular shelving unit
by Studio MVW (self-production), 2016

Xiangsheng II console
by Studio MVW (self-production), 2016

SHANGHAI ROSE

Shanghai boasts a number of landmark Art Deco buildings from the 1920s and 1930s, when the city was famously known as the 'Paris of the East'. Today, Studio MVW, based in the city's fashionable and historic French concession area, channels the 'Shanghai Rose' glamour of that heady era with exclusive design-art furniture that is not only functionally and aesthetically innovative, but also exquisitely executed. Their limited-edition Jinshi series, for instance, has a strong Postmodern Neo-Deco feel, while the literal translation of its title is 'Gold Stone'. Using a combination of Burmese pink jade and anodized stainless-steel coloured in an attractive rose-gold brass, the series, with its gravity-defying coffee table, elegant boudoir-style consoles and range of eye-catching lights, cleverly balances a strict minimalistic formalism with the sensuality of the pink jade, which is internally lit to accentuate its soft-glowing, rose-tinted beauty.

JINSHI PINK JADE COFFEE TABLE #1
by Studio MVW
(self-production), 2017

↤
JINSHI PINK JADE WALL LIGHT #2
by Studio MVW
(self-production), 2017

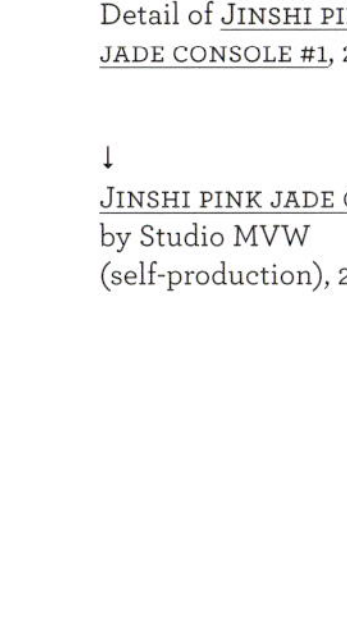

THE BLOOMING SERIES

Studio MVW's Blooming series is a playful Neo-Postmodern reimagining of the classical Ming vase. Each of the designs in the series features this well-known, archetypal Chinese form, which opens up or 'blooms' to reveal its intended function as a cabinet, console or suspended ceiling light. Made of stainless steel, the vases are lacquered a deep blue, redolent of the inky hue used on historic blue-and-white Chinese porcelain, but when opened they reveal secret receptacles lacquered in immaculate white. Strikingly contrasting straight lines with soft curves, these pieces provide a rare element of surprise and performance. This series also reveals Xu Ming and Virgine Moriette's skilful cross-cultural interpretation of forms, which playfully subvert their historic cultural associations.

Blooming ceiling light #1
by Studio MVW
(self-production), 2017

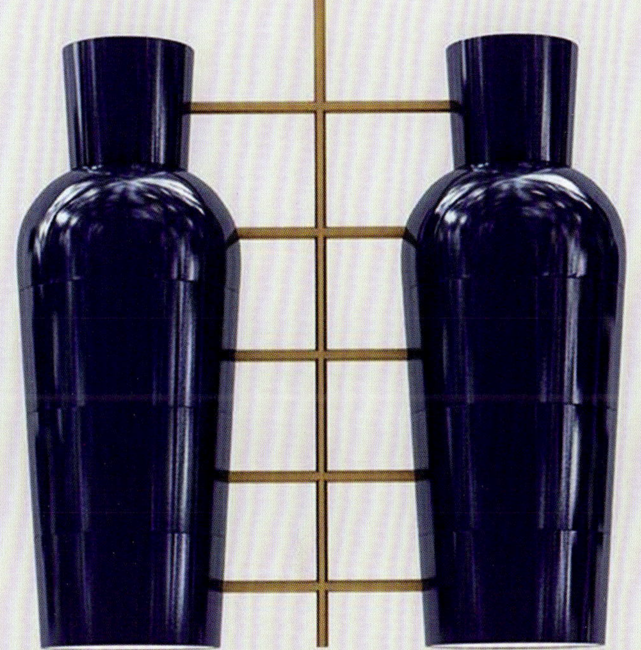

Forest poufs
by Sherry Xu
for 8 Hour, 2017

PLAYFUL + SIMPLE

Sherry Xu studied art and design at the Shanghai Academy of Fine Arts, and then spent over a decade gaining experience in designing and making furniture. In 2015 she founded her own company, 8 Hour, to manufacture her own designs for furniture and homewares. Its name, reflecting the eight hours of an average workday, sums up her desire to find innovative and playful solutions for the requirements of everyday living. Her Timeline table, for example, has an inclined base featuring continuous and broken lines made up of metal rods, which are intended to symbolize the flow and continuity of time. But more than this, when the table is seen from different angles, it has a playful, kinetic Op Art quality. Likewise, Xu's variously sized Forest poufs are intended to inject a bit of visual vitality into office and domestic environments. Easy to move, the pieces are meant to be combined at will to create functional sculptural compositions within the spaces they occupy. As Xu observes, her goal is 'to find surprises in everyday moments and create products that make life more interesting.'

OTHERWORLDLY MONOLITHS

It is obvious that the place at which designers choose to study and the field in which they opt to train always have a massive impact on the design approach they later adopt in professional practice. Look, for instance, at Yang Hongjie, who took a master's degree in contextual design at the Design Academy Eindhoven, which is famous for its promotion of experimental design research, and for encouraging provocative conceptual design that pushes the boundaries of the discipline. Yang's chosen area of academic specialization, contextual design, is as the name suggests all about exploring the larger societal context of design and its practice. It should, then, come as no surprise that, since completing his studies, Yang has focused on creating work that, as he puts it, 'examines where the distinctions in nature blur between intervention and non-intervention, as intervention itself starts to be seen as part of a natural process'. His otherworldly Monolith series, for example, is all about the concept of metamorphosis, for, as he observes, 'It is through transformation that we find enlightenment'. These one-off and limited-edition pieces, sculpted from aluminium, stainless steel or bronze, have a metallic, rubble-like appearance, which is playfully contrasted with their integral mirrored surfaces. Monumental in its raw sculptural presence, this limited-edition design-art collection possesses an aesthetic that seems to mystically transcend the divisions between the man-made and natural worlds, and belong instead to an otherworldly realm. Indeed, Yang believes that 'Nature as we know it is coming to an end', for, if you think about it, almost everywhere in the world is to a greater or lesser extent touched by the impact of humankind.

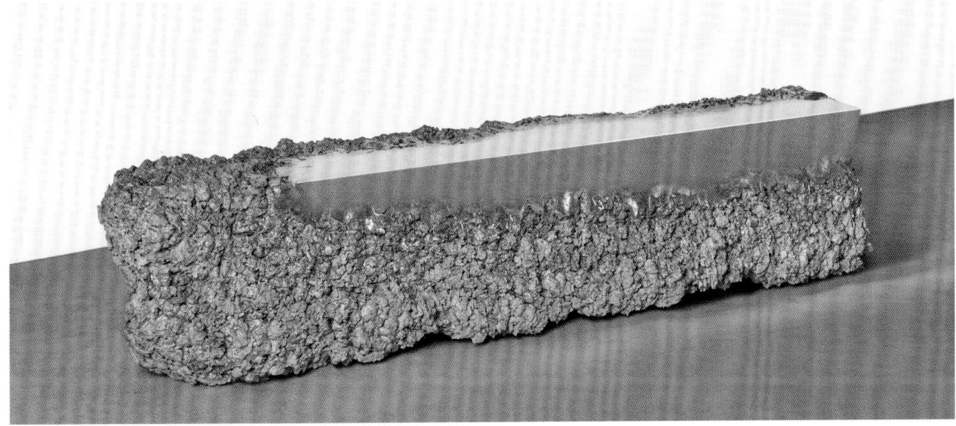

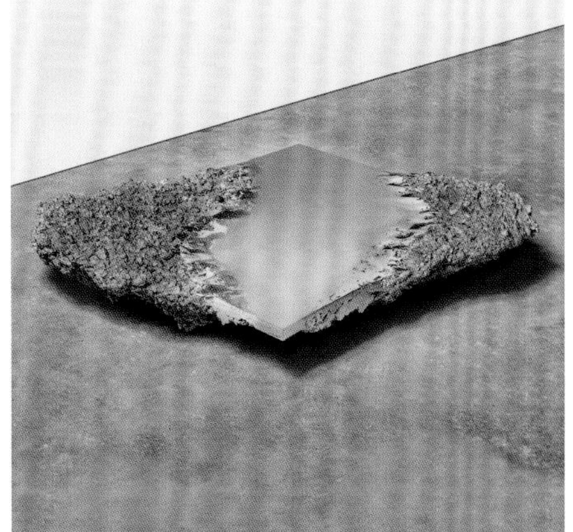

←
<u>Synthesis Monolith stainless-steel stool</u>
by Yang Hongjie for Gallery ALL,
2018

↑
<u>Synthesis Monolith aluminium bench</u>
by Yang Hongjie for Gallery ALL,
2017

↗
<u>Synthesis Monolith aluminium coffee table</u>
by Yang Hongjie for Gallery ALL,
2017 – a one-off piece

→
Detail of Synthesis Monolith
aluminium bench

PHILIP YAP/TANG TANG + ZHANG YING/LANDWOOD

NEO-DECO ORIENTALISM

The establishment of the lifestyle brand Landwood (aka Nangu in Chinese) was inspired by its founders' shared love of woodcraft. Zhang Ying is a designer, who studied at the Queensland College of Art in Australia , while her co-founder Jin Ping is a well-known art photographer, who has a special interest in nature, culture and their interaction. As Landwood's artistic director, Zhang recognizes that design is fundamentally about life, and that at its core is the relationship between use and beauty. As she explains, 'I believe that the secret to creating beautiful objects lies in harnessing the energy and elements that nature has generously provided for us.' Her stunning Bread armchair, with its deep cushioned base, does indeed look rather like a loaf of bread rising in a tin, and elegantly showcases the beauty of the wood used in its construction. This is achieved by using Ming-derived forms, while at the same time evoking the stylishness of 1920s' Shanghai Art Deco. The gently embracing arms of this distinctive seating design give it an emotionally engaging appeal, while its yellow upholstery has overt imperial connotations, as in the past only emperors were allowed to wear that colour. Based in China, the awarding-winning Malaysian designer Philip Yap has likewise created various furniture pieces for his own fusion-design brand, Tang Tang, that playfully reference Ming furniture in a stylish Neo-Deco way. His translation of traditional Chinese forms and motifs into designs with a strong Postmodern aesthetic, such as his My Fair Lady armchair and Dynasty room divider, reveal the rising stylistic exuberance of New Chinese Design.

←

by Philip Yap
for Tang Tang, 2015

↑
My fair lady round-backed chair
by Philip Yap
for Tang Tang, 2016

↓ & →
Bread armchair
by Zhang Ying
for Landwood, 2016 – also known
as the Heshe armchair

YUAN YUAN/RUYI

A LIFE-ENRICHING TOMORROW

When most people talk about classical Chinese furniture, they are invariably referring to the Ming and Qing dynasties. That's because so few examples of furniture have survived from the earlier Song dynasty. Certainly, as many of the furniture designs in this book attest, much stylistic inspiration is being derived by today's Chinese designers from the archetypal forms of the Ming and Qing dynasties. The founder of Ruyi, Yuan Yuan, however, thinks the obsession with these historic furniture forms is a mistake because they tend to reflect a combination of Confucianism and Manchu imperial power, and therefore represent only a very small element of Chinese culture. In terms of her own highly sculptural designs, Yuan prefers to draw inspiration from a wider cultural landscape in order to create work that references ancient and traditional Chinese themes while also being perfectly suited to today's lifestyles. Her goal is to build a more internationally appealing language of contemporary Chinese design that will enrich people's lives. Her Light Fan screen cleverly incorporates traditional rigid, scallop-shaped fans into its construction, while Chinese folding fans, which are symbolic of the cultivation and refined taste of ancient Chinese scholars, inspired the form of her Phoenix Fan chair (overleaf). Her Stone Vision chaise longue also references literati culture, in that interestingly shaped rocks, known as *gonshi*, were traditionally used for contemplative purposes by scholars and were considered essential items in their study rooms.

→
Light fan screen
by Yuan Yuan for Ruyi, 2015

↓
Stone vision chaise longue,
stone vision armchair and
water lily coffee table
by Yuan Yuan for Ruyi, 2015

EVOCATIVE SHAPES

The young Chinese designer Yuan Yuan launched her own lifestyle brand, Ruyi, in 2015 and that same year showed her first furniture collection at the Salone del Mobile in Milan. The name of her company is a play on words: in Chinese *ru yi* means 'just like tomorrow or the future', while *ruyi*, which is pronounced the same way, means 'as you wish', and refers to the S-shaped ceremonial sceptres of Chinese Buddhism, as well as to a talisman meant to bring good fortune. The company name therefore alludes to both the past and the future. This accords with Yuan's belief that a crucial balance needs to be struck between the age-old traditions of the East and the universalism of international contemporary design. She understands that strict adherence to cultural traditions can all too easily restrict creativity, yet is also mindful that globalization can lead design to lose its sense of 'local' relevance. Yuan is married to a sculptor, and her work exudes a formal sculptural confidence that is quintessentially modern yet inspired by Chinese cultural roots. Her Forward chair, with its deeply upholstered seat, references the throne-like chairs used in the imperial court, while her pebble-like Shoal screen and her mountain-echoing Stone Legend sofa are inspired by the strong connection between Chinese culture and the natural world. As Yuan explains, 'I believe nature is an enduring theme that serves as a bridge between the past and the future, the East and the West.' Her goal with Ruyi is to span those time and national gaps within the realm of furniture design.

↑
STONE LEGEND SOFA
by Yuan Yuan for Ruyi, 2017

←
PHOENIX FAN CHAIR
by Yuan Yuan for Ruyi, 2015

↑
FORWARD ARMCHAIR
by Yuan Yuan for Ruyi, 2017

→
SHOAL SCREEN
by Yuan Yuan for Ruyi, 2017

CHINESE SCHOLAR CULTURE

For those in the West, it is quite diffi-cult to understand Chinese consumers' attachment to rare tropical hardwoods, especially rosewood, but, as one Chinese design commentator remarked to us, 'It is not just furniture, it is culture.' In fact, the history of rosewood furniture in China goes back to at least the tenth century, although it reached its apotheosis during the Ming dynasty thanks to the introduc-tion of innovative joinery techniques. That said, furnishing tastes in China are rap-idly changing. For instance, the popularity of elaborately carved *hongmu* furniture, as well as bulky baroque-style and showy 'tycoon'-style rosewood furniture, has nosedived in recent years, with blonder woods becoming increasingly popular, especially among younger, design-savvy consumers. The taste for a more contem-porary look that channels the so-called lit-erati aesthetic associated with the refined lifestyle tastes of scholars of the Song and Ming periods and uses fewer materials in its construction is also growing. This change is demonstrated by the designs produced by Yuè Literati, which was founded by the designer Xu Hui. The com-pany's sales director, who is highly mind-ful of the ecological debate surrounding the use of rosewood, notes, 'This simpler style of design uses far less rosewood than is used to make traditional-style furniture. For us as furniture producers, the Ming style embodies the spirit of China and the long tradition of scholars who don't pursue power or money, but beauty.' Nonetheless, rosewood is a precious natural resource that needs greater protection and should never be mindlessly squandered on poor design. The only way to make it sustaina-ble is to restrict its supply so that only the very best, most considerate designers are allowed to work with it.

PLUM BLOSSOM CABINET
by Xu Hui for Yuè Literati/
Yizhishang, 2018

↑
WISDOM TABLE
by Xu Hui for Yuè Literati/
Yizhishang, 2018

←
SWAN TABLE
by Xu Hui for Yuè Literati/
Yizhishang, 2018

ZHANG ZHOUJIE

CUTTING-EDGE SEATING SERIES

One of the great pioneers of contemporary Chinese design, Zhang Zhoujie is at the very forefront of professional practice, using revolutionary and disruptive computer algorithms to create furniture unlike anything ever seen before. Indeed, his furniture is not actually designed by him per se, but by the generative computer algorithms that he and his team create. For over a decade Zhang has been working on his evolving Digital Object/ Triangulation Series, which is inspired as much by the Taoist philosophy of spontaneity as it is by the Parametricism movement, which he first encountered as a visiting researcher at London's Architectural Association in 2009. The series comprises various designs, including chairs, stools and tables, the forms of which have been worked out by computer software based on parameters established by Zhang, involving basic maths logic, such as dimensions and the movement of points. The programme then grows a design from a two-dimensional plane into a three-dimensional form. This formal data is used to flawlessly hand-weld the physical limited-edition designs in brass or stainless steel. These origami-like designs have a distinctive fractal beauty, which is futuristic and thought-provoking.

↑
Early testing models in paper, 2009

↗
Early computer-generation program, 2010

→
<u>OBJECT # SQN1-F2 A CHAIR</u>
by Zhang Zhoujie
(self-production), 2011

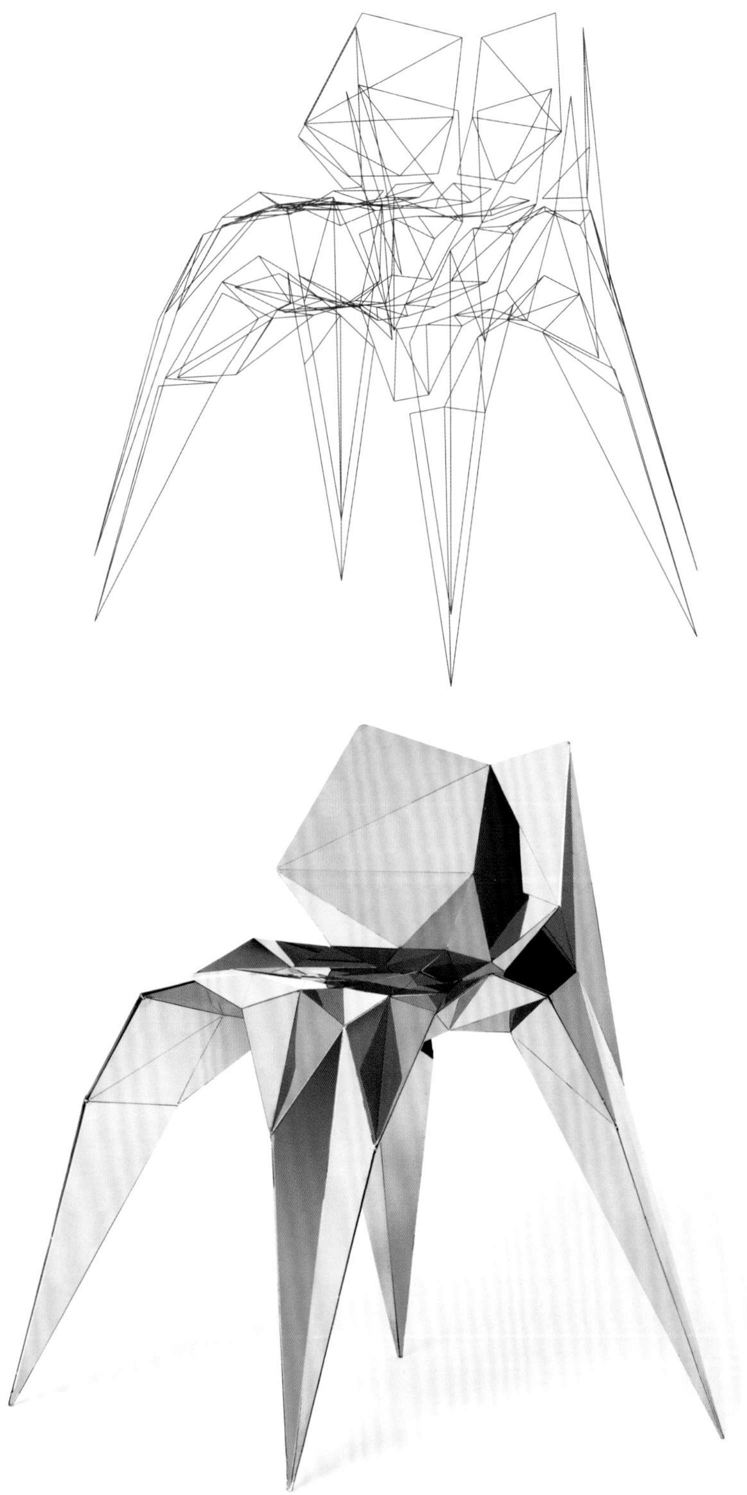

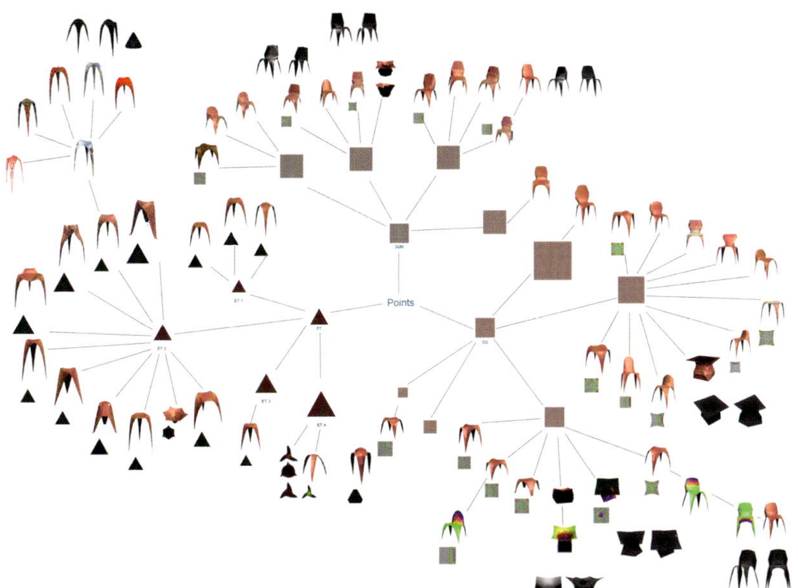

Points

←
'The Object Evolution Tree'
computer algorithm data map, 2009

↓
OBJECT # SQN3-A CHAIR
by Zhang Zhoujie
(self-production), 2011

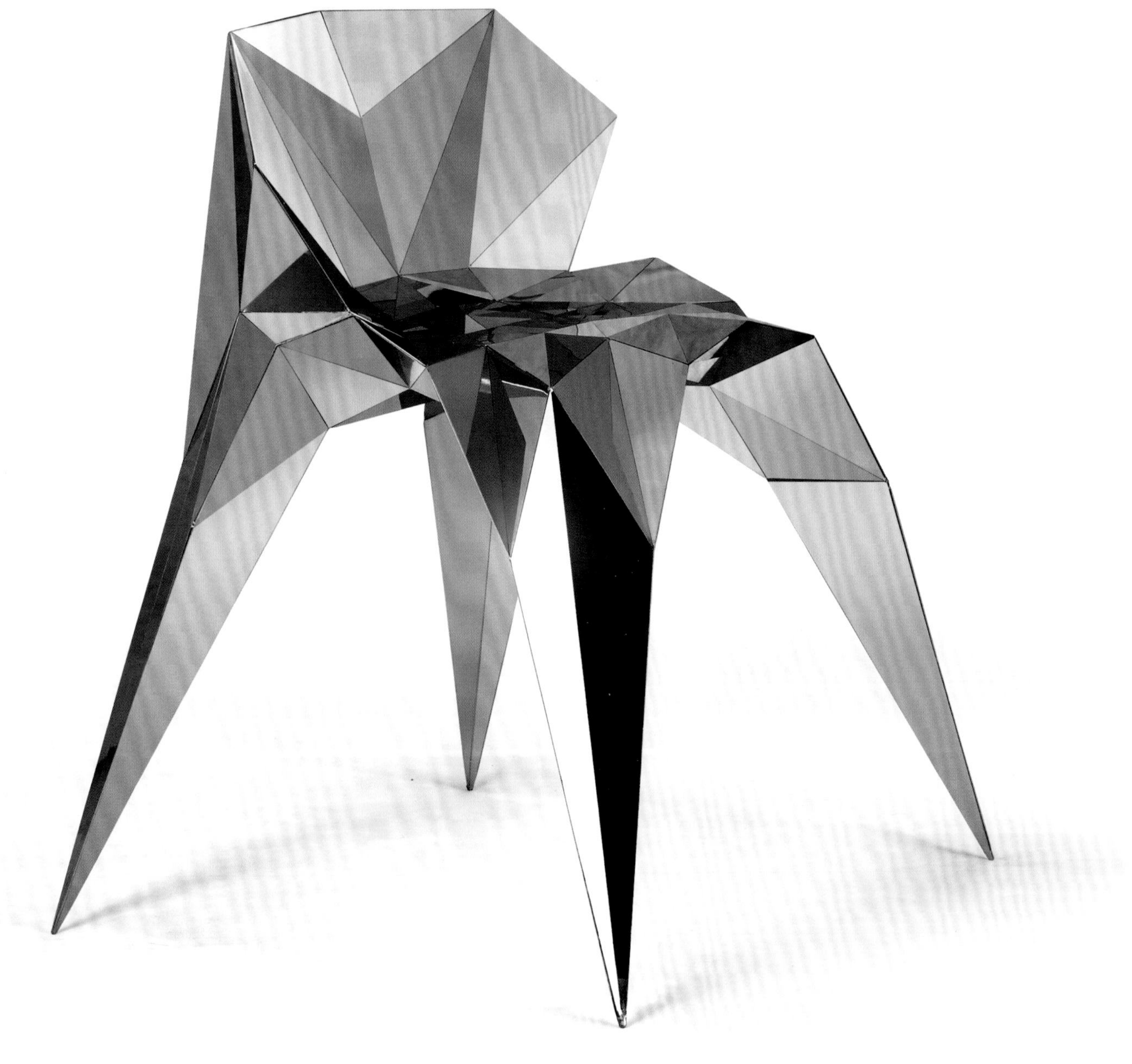

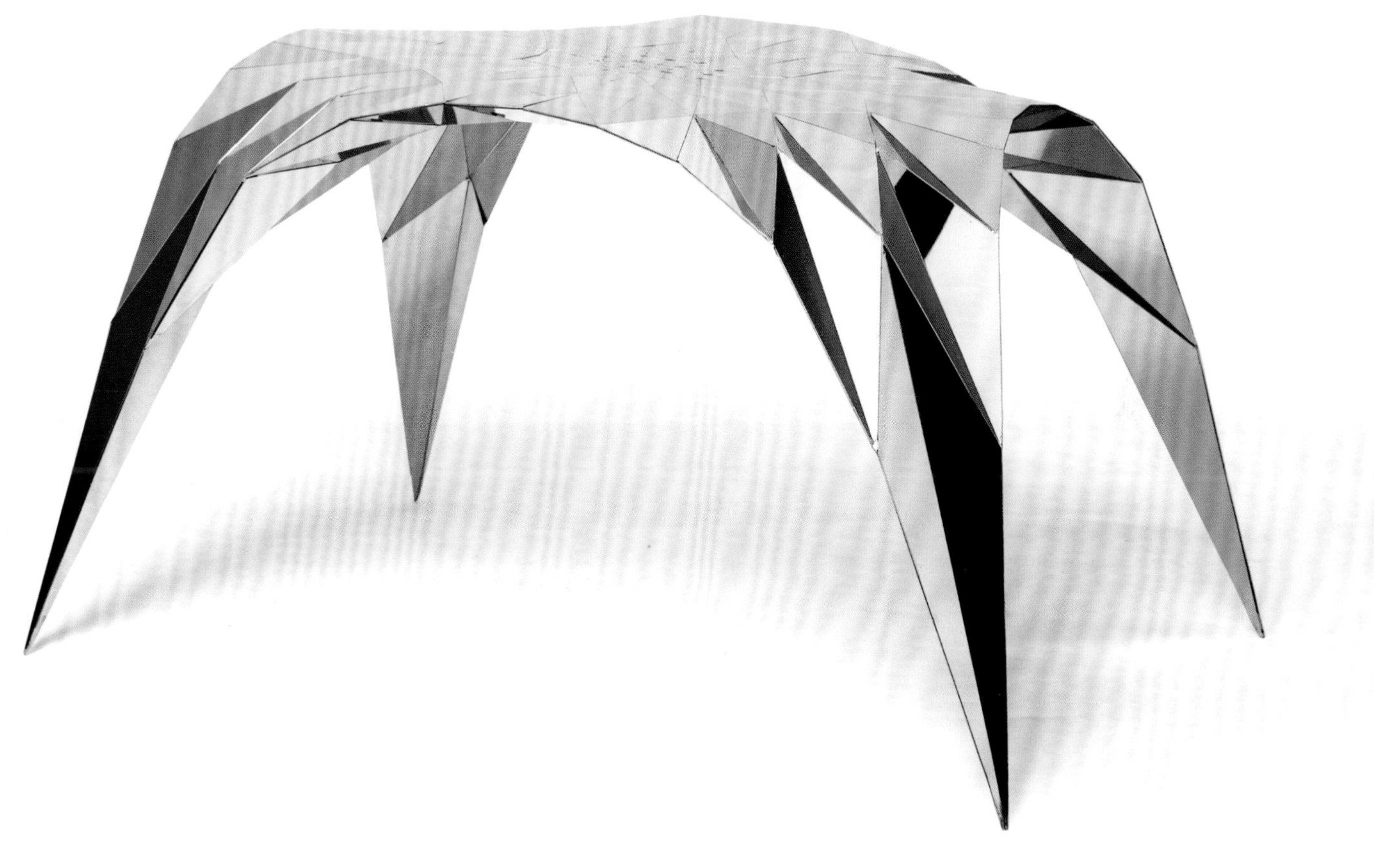

A NEW FACET OF DESIGN

This beautiful table and bench, with their complex faceted surfaces, are perfect examples of Zhang Zhoujie's 'philosophy of actionless', whereby the digital planes of a design are first sucked inwards and then allowed to expand outwards with a natural tendency. As Zhoujie explains of the table, 'The [design] process only took a few seconds, but the continuous logical deductions behind it took over three years.' The aim was to perfectly combine design function with a naturalistic growth process using computer algorithms that would expose 'the natural beauty of digital logic'. Once the designs had been digitally generated by the computer, it took another three months to painstakingly translate them, using handcraft methods, into beautiful, otherworldly limited-edition furniture available in either stainless steel or brass.

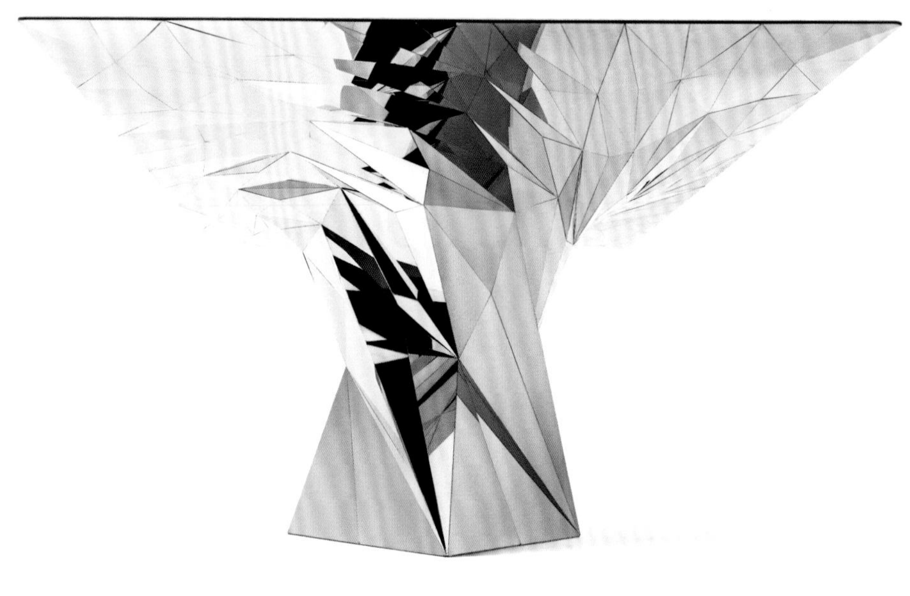

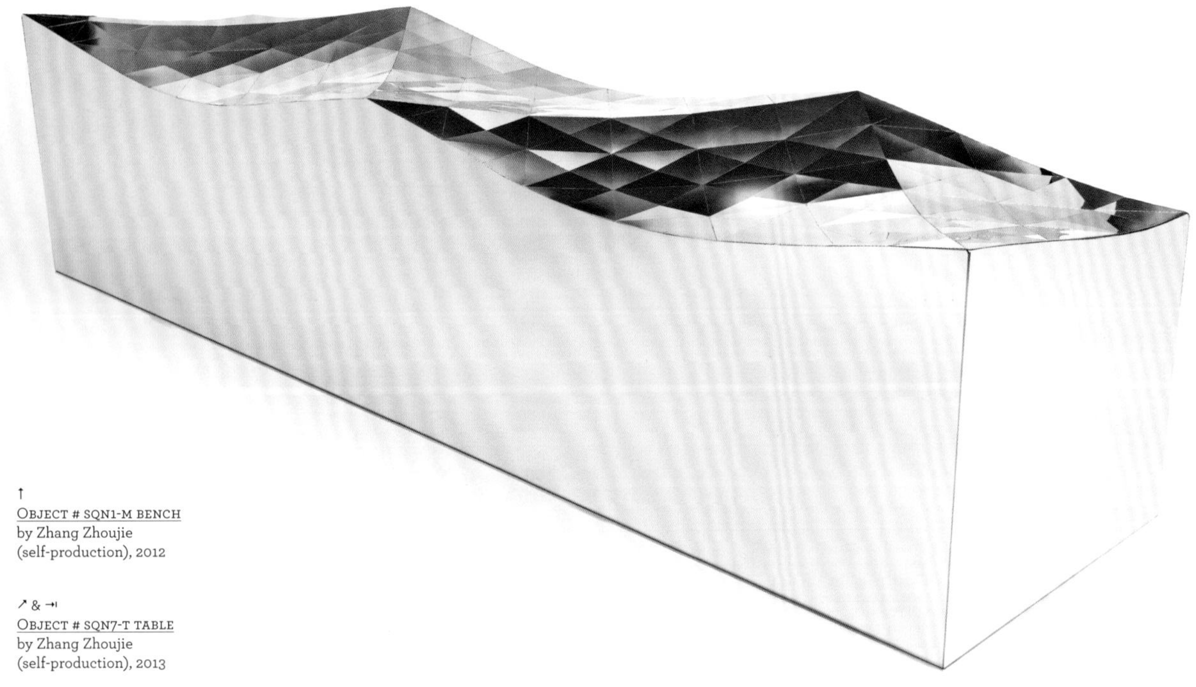

↑
OBJECT # SQN1-M BENCH
by Zhang Zhoujie
(self-production), 2012

↗ & →
OBJECT # SQN7-T TABLE
by Zhang Zhoujie
(self-production), 2013

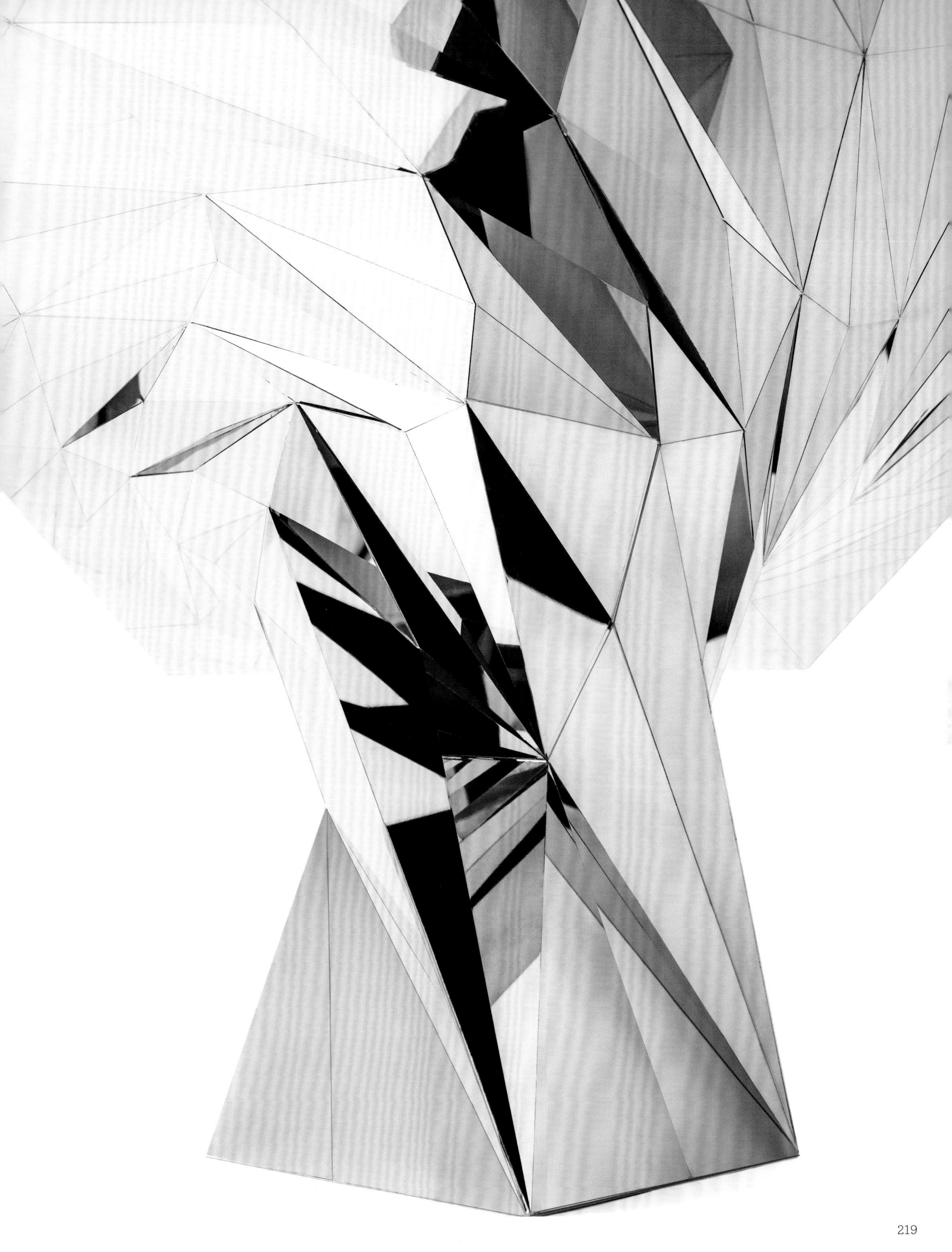

THE SOUL OF WOOD

In 2005 Zheng Zhilong moved 400 miles from his hometown in order to study architecture and environmental art in Guangzhou. At that time Guangzhou College Town was still under construction, and there were derelict and demolished houses everywhere, with their unloved and unwanted contents scattered among the building debris. One of the courses Zheng was taking at college required him to find objects within these mounds of slum-clearance waste to use as the basis of a research project. During his searches, he saw over and over again discarded yet perfectly serviceable logs, planks and other wooden items that had been simply left out to rot. Shocked by the sheer waste of this, he began collecting any potentially reusable wood he came across, and by the time of his graduation had accumulated 5 tonnes of it. As the rescued material continued to pile up, Zheng decided, in 2013, to establish his own studio, Shimuji, which in Chinese means 'pick up wood'. The plan was to transform his collection of old wood into new furniture – to bring abandoned materials back to life, and, if 'the wood has a soul', to rekindle it in his designs, which are inspired by forms found in nature. His Tree chair, which skilfully combines found walnut, burr birch and maple in its construction, was selected as one of the finalists for the prestigious Loewe Craft Prize in 2017. This simple yet characterful piece exemplifies Zheng's ethical approach to design and making. Directly inspired by the origin of the woods used in its construction, its branching back and legs seemingly evoke the spirit trees from Chinese mythology and folklore.

→|
Shan shou bench and stool
by Zheng Zhilong
for Shimuji, 2015

←
Tree chair
by Zheng Zhilong
for Shimuji, 2015

→|
Mushroom stools
by Zheng Zhilong
for Shimuji, 2016

ZHONG SONG

THE CLASSICAL REIMAGINED

Zhong Song is a highly respected artist and designer, who studied sculpture at the Central Academy of Fine Arts in Beijing, graduating in 1999. After his studies, he established Zhongsong Design and has since worked across a wide variety of creative disciplines, including architecture, interior design, public art and product design. Although he is determined not to limit himself to one specific discipline, most of his time is dedicated to designing interiors and furniture. In 2010 he founded two brands, Wanwu and Tianwu, with the aim of promoting more 'peaceful and balanced' lifestyles. The installations shown here, which Zhong devised for two exhibitions, held in Beijing and Hangzhou respectively, incorporate long and low tea tables plus low cushioned seating, which allude to the refined lifestyle of the Song dynasty. Yet, despite their evocations of the past, these 'rooms' are also inspired by today's growing interest in well-being, for they are all about creating environments that enable people to savour the sensorial moment, which is so key to the enjoyment of China's thriving tea culture.

Ancient and Present Dreams installation
by Zhong Song at the 'Camellia Sinensis: Life in a Plant' exhibition, organized by China Academy of Art at the Folk Art Museum in Hangzhou, 2016

FORGOTTEN CLASSICS INSTALLATION
by Zhong Song at the 'Forgotten Classics'
exhibition, curated by Xia Jifeng and organized
by Hive Centre for Contemporary Art, 2017

KIRAN ZHU/ZIINLIFE

BOLD FORMS

The origins of ziinlife go back to 2010, when Kiran Zhu, having recently returned from studying overseas, began collaborating with fellow founder Lily Yang. Their shared dream was to establish their own lifestyle brand, which would offer accessible, affordable and well-designed furniture that was intended to enhance the everyday lives of ordinary people. They eventually founded ziinlife in 2013, with Kiran acting as chief designer, and Yang being in charge of day-to-day operations. Since then, the company has gone from strength to strength, thanks to its focus on furniture for young consumers, who tend to live in smaller living spaces than older people. Ziinlife's quirky Pea Pod sofa (inspired by the Minions from the *Despicable Me* series of films) and its elegant Fluid sofa, for example, have scaled-down proportions perfectly suited to compact apartments. Likewise, the Enlight cabinet was designed not only for multifunctional storage, but also to emphasize the passage of natural light during the day in order to enliven a room, however dark or small it might be. The retro-styled Nifty armchair projects a similarly light-hearted aesthetic that is also intended to cheer up living spaces. Its eye-catching yet simple form looks as though it might have been lifted straight out of a cartoon, while the Merge rocking chair when set in motion provides a modicum of playful interaction. Kiran Zhu's aim is to create designs that are 'full of delight, wonder and surprise', and so far, this has proved to be an award-winning formula.

↓
FLUID SOFA
by Kiran Zhu
for ziinlife, 2018

↓
NIFTY ARMCHAIR
by Kiran Zhu
for ziinlife, 2013

↘
ENLIGHT CABINET
by Kiran Zhu
for ziinlife, 2015

↑
Pea pod sofa – 'minion' collection
by Kiran Zhu
for ziinlife, 2018

→
Merge rocking chair
by Kiran Zhu
for ziinlife, 2018

225

ELEGANT DESIGNS
FOR SMALL SPACES

Ziinlife's byline for its catalogue from 2017 was 'design for our times', which perfectly sums up the company's focus on generating real-need furnishing solutions. Having identified that there is a very large demographic of young Chinese people setting up their first homes, the company specializes in producing well-designed and affordable furniture for them. The company's chief designer, Kiran Zhu, understands that space in starter homes is often at a premium, so he incorporates as much functionality as possible into his furniture. While some of ziinlife's designs have an exuberant, youthful air, others are more restrained in their aesthetic. For instance, the Flow tea table and the 1 + 1 folding bench, although possessing playful and unconventional constructions, also have a definable sophistication. His Infinity cabinets are likewise highly considered in terms of their restrained yet elegant look and space-saving functionality. Made up of modular units, they can be mixed and matched depending on the required use – bedside cabinets, sideboards, bookcases and so forth. The main idea is that people might start off with just a few of the units, then add to them as their furnishing needs change and grow. It is, however, the Gentle dresser that perhaps best expresses ziinlife's pursuit of space-saving perfection. Despite its diminutive proportions and slender depth, this stylish minimalist design incorporates a drawer and has an integrated light around the mirror, and even cleverly references the well-known Chinese circle-in-a-square motif, which symbolizes heaven and earth.

→|
FLOW TEA TABLE
by Kiran Zhu
for ziinlife, 2018

↓↘
1 + 1 FOLDING BENCH
by Kiran Zhu
for ziinlife, 2018

→|
GENTLE DRESSER
by Kiran Zhu
for ziinlife, 2018

⇥|
INFINITY CABINETS
by Kiran Zhu
for ziinlife, 2018

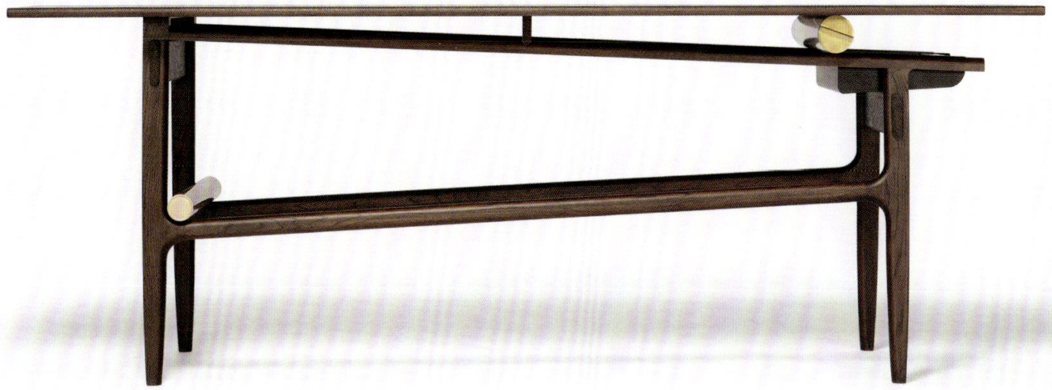

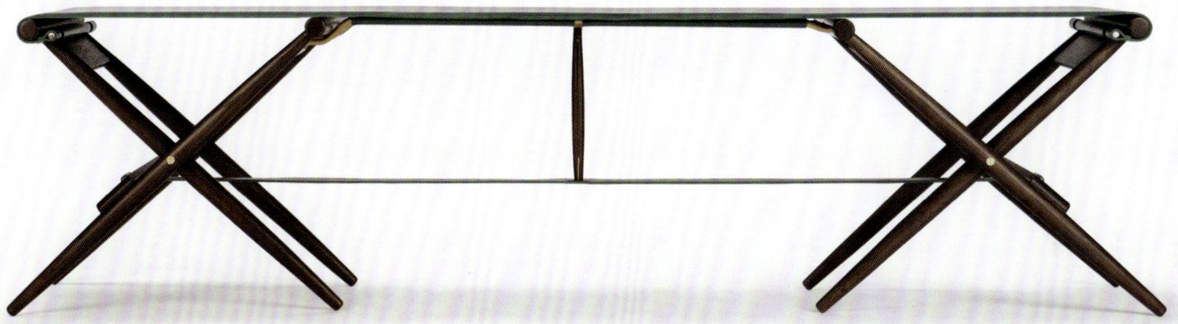

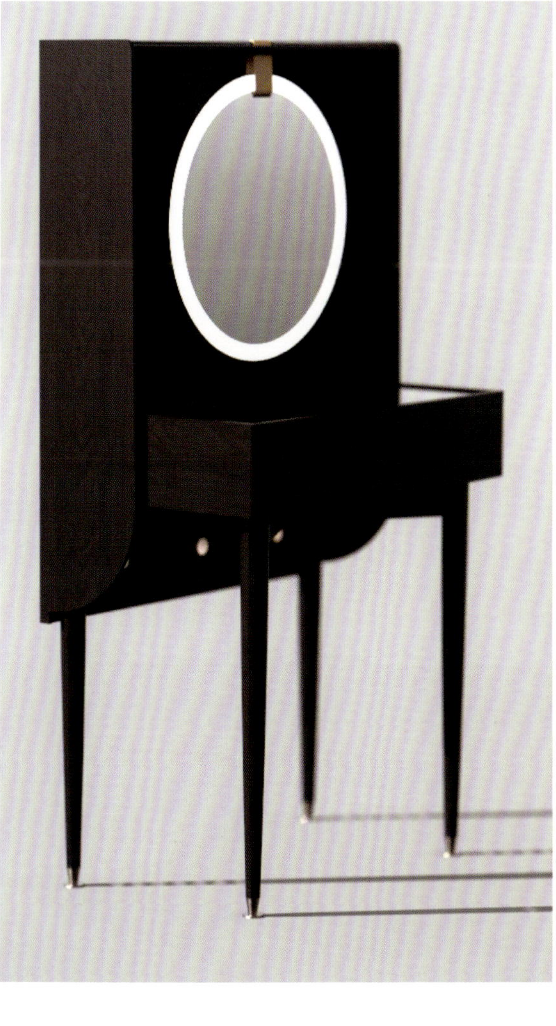

JUST A CRAFTSMAN FROM CHINA

Zhu Xiaojie modestly describes himself as 'Just a craftsman from China', but he is actually one of the country's most celebrated designers and an important pioneer of New Chinese Design. He is also the founder of his own furniture brand, Opal Furniture, and the principal of his Wenzhou Furniture School. While he initially made his name as a furniture designer, his creative endeavours have expanded to include, among other things, architecture, lighting and ceramics. Nonetheless, it is his furniture for which he is still best known. His beautiful chairs, tables, stools and benches generally have an overt 'woody' aesthetic, and incorporate beautifully grained timbers to stunning effect. As Zhu explains, 'Traditional Chinese art stresses the use of line, be it in calligraphy or Chinese painting, and so does the furniture of the Ming dynasty with its pleasing smoothness and rounded arcs. I want to express this spirit in my own designs.' The beautiful flowing forms that distinguish his furniture, which is manufactured using both handcrafts and high-tech methods of production, are inspired by the traditional furniture of both the Song and Ming dynasties, and by the natural beauty of the materials used in their construction. Zhu's modern interpretations of ancient Chinese furniture forms were first exhibited abroad at the Cologne International Furniture Exhibition in 2009, and soon afterwards he was invited to produce various designs for the 2010 Shanghai World Expo. The resultant 300 furniture pieces famously showcased more than 80 different styles associated with Chinese cultural traditions.

↤
BUTTERFLY BENCH
by Zhu Xiaojie (2002) at his Opal Furniture
Studio in Wenzhou, which has been described
by *AD* magazine as 'the most beautiful home
in the world'

THE CHINESE WOODSMAN

One of the key characteristics of Zhu Xiaojie's furniture is his use of slab-like, end-grain timbers that reveal the tree rings. The thick slices of trunk he uses for his tabletops come from dead trees that are 100 or more years old. By repurposing their wood in this way, he is effectively giving these trees a new lease of life, and believes that their spirit or character is thereby passed on. But even more than this, these cross-sections of wood can bestow beautiful surprises. As Zhu observes, 'unique design sometimes comes from unexpected events'. While making his Couple tea table, for example, its top split into two pieces that resembled the traditional Chinese symbols for yin and yang. While the craftsmen in his workshop began discussing how to repair this break, Zhu instead decided to keep it, for then the table would 'display its most original and natural condition, while the symbolic language created by chance would be retained'. Zhu's adherence to Taoist philosophy and his enduring love of wood are powerfully revealed in his furniture pieces, which are fundamentally three-dimensional celebrations of the natural world's inherent beauty and the exquisite aesthetic value gained from perpetuating a culture of skilled handcrafting.

↖
COUPLE TEA TABLE
by Zhu Xiaojie
for Opal Furniture, 2004

↖
PEBBLE TEA TABLE
by Zhu Xiaojie
for Opal Furniture, 2008

←
MUSHROOM STOOL
by Zhu Xiaojie
for Opal Furniture, 2018

→|
Detail of Forest table at Zhu Xiaojie's
Opal Furniture Studio in Wenzhou, 2002

GEO-MING

The Chinese designer Zhu Zi founded the Suyab Design Company at the Guangzhou Academy of Fine Arts in 2003. The studio was named after the ancient Silk Road city, which is now in Kyrgyzstan. This choice of name was an early expression of interest in China's ancient past, and especially its historically significant trading links. Such interest has since grown widely in China. Indeed, it is central to the whole New Chinese Design phenomenon, which takes pride in the nation's remarkable cultural traditions and seeks to revitalize them. To this end, Zhu established the Suyab furniture company in 2015 to manufacture and distribute his own designs. Although his work is, as he puts it, 'grounded in the contemporary and explores the aesthetics of everyday functionality', it also relies on 'the soul of craftsmanship'. Incorporating exquisitely grained marbles, high-quality leather and beautiful woods, Zhu's designs reflect the Chinese obsession with high-end luxury materials, yet the forms he uses are refreshingly contemporary in their aesthetic reductivism and geometric restraint.

←
TREE TEA TABLE
by Zhu Zi for Suyab, 2017

→
FOLDING LINE ARMCHAIR
by Zhu Zi for Suyab, 2015

↓
A BAND SIDEBOARD
by Zhu Zi for Suyab, 2018

WARM-TONED LUXURY

Like so many of the leading furniture brands in China, Suyab – or Sui Ji, as it is known in Chinese – evolved out of a successful interior-design studio. It arose from Zhu Zi's Suyab Design Company, which specialized in the interior design of luxury villas, for which it would often create bespoke furniture. It was a natural progression for Zhu to expand on this type of work by founding his own high-end furniture manufacturing company in 2015. His aim was to create pieces with a distinctive originality and oriental aesthetic suited to modern lifestyles. Much of his furniture exudes a sense of warm-toned luxury, which reflects the Asian preference for warmer and richer colour palettes when it comes to home decoration, while at the same time his designs reference Chinese materials and motifs. His In-Between tea table, for instance, incorporates a top made of glass blocks that look like slabs of amber, a nod to the ancient Chinese belief that amber was composed of fossilized tiger tears, which encapsulated the courage of these big cats. By contrast, the back section of his dark wood and leather Song armchair playfully takes the form of a giant abacus, while his circular display cabinet, with its small, light-filtering gap, symbolically evokes 'the circle of heaven'.

↑
A CIRCLE DISPLAY CABINET
by Zhu Zi for Suyab, 2018

→
SONG ARMCHAIR
by Zhu Zi for Suyab, 2015

→|
IN-BETWEEN TEA TABLE
by Zhu Zi for Suyab, 2018

TWENTY-FIVE YEARS OF FURNITURE CHINA

Over the last two and a half decades, the China International Furniture Expo – otherwise known as Furniture China – has helped to promote the incredible new wave of Chinese furniture design, the best examples of which have been so beautifully showcased in the pages of this book. Indeed, such is the technical skill and aesthetic innovation found in these works that China's furniture designers are becoming frequent award winners in international design competitions. As the market leader within China's furniture-related exhibition sector, Furniture China is playing a vital role in nurturing and publicizing this new and exciting era in contemporary Chinese furniture design. By adhering to its stated policy of 'export orientation, high-end domestic sales, original design and industry guidance', Furniture China provides an important platform for showcasing and trading home furniture, contract furnishings and a wide array of raw materials. It attracts ever-increasing numbers of exhibitors and visitors from all over the world, so it's little wonder that Furniture China has become one of the largest shows of its kind, and exerts a strong international influence throughout the world.

The Amazing Success of Furniture China

In the second week of September every year, all kinds of superior furniture products from around globe are showcased at Furniture China, which is visited by professional buyers, designers and consumers alike. In fact, the 2018 exhibition achieved a new record in terms of visitor numbers: 166,479 visits were made by buyers or visitors from 132 different countries and regions over the show's four-day duration. This was up 9.82 per cent on the previous year, and probably attributable to a marked increase in overseas visitors. A total of 21,218 visits (an increase of 23.87 per cent) were made by visitors from Europe, the USA, South Korea, Japan and Australia, all of which have enjoyed long-term cooperation with the Chinese market.

Since its inception in 1993, Furniture China has enjoyed constant and rapid growth. In terms of scale, it has grown from an initial 3,000 square metres to 350,000 square metres, covering two venues – SNIEC (for Furniture China) and SWEECC (for Maison Shanghai) that are interconnected with city-wide design activities under Shanghai Home Design Week. Our International Brand Halls, Contemporary Design Halls, Contemporary Furniture Halls and FMC Halls have become important places for visitors, and their interest has in turn attracted many more domestic and overseas enterprises to exhibit. Furniture China 2018 showcased a total of 3,500 high-quality domestic and overseas furniture brands from 155 different countries and regions. Of these, 1,342 were contemporary home furniture brands, 129 were home-grown design brands, and 220 were overseas brands. This vast and international platform is unique to Furniture China, but it did not happen overnight. Over the last 25 years, Furniture China has closely followed market trends but more recently has increasingly placed importance on innovation, and this has led to major shifts and transformations in its structure. In the future, has stated Wang Mingliang, founder and director of Shanghai UBM Sinoepxo International Exhibition Co. Ltd., Furniture China will focus on quality rather than quantity, the aim being to create a first-class international furniture show.

A New Platform for a New Wave of Chinese Brands

In recent years, Furniture China has provided a very important platform for Chinese furniture to develop from 'copy + manufacture' to 'design + innovation'. In fact, since 2011 the show's aim has been to cultivate, support and foster original Chinese design. This has yielded very positive results, with a number of original furniture brands – such as U*, DOMO, ziinlife, Pusu and shiershiman – having taken root and blossomed. At present, Furniture China has three huge design halls dedicated to both high-end and mainstream manufacturers, as well as several smaller spaces where younger designers, start-up brands and other furniture-related ventures can show off their wares. The latter have facilitated greater cooperation between different enterprises leading to an increase in opportunities for all parties and ultimately more contracts being signed.

A brand new initiative, Creation of Creators (COC), was launched at Furniture China in 2018. This new platform – jointly initiated by the businessman Wang Mingliang and the designer Frank Chou (Zhou Chenchen) – aims to promote a holistic approach and 'ecological ethos' that will help the Chinese design industry to integrate more eco-friendly policies. COC will focus not only on design, but also on resources, design management and the interconnection of innovative ideas in order to publicize, showcase and ultimately help shape brand identities.

In addition, Furniture China is committed to safeguarding the interests of those brands and designers that use traditional methods and technology. The Gold Idea Award, launched in 2014, and the Innovation Award, established in

Main entrance hall of the China International Furniture Expo in Pudong, Shanghai, 2018

2000, have both helped to cultivate innovation in China's furniture industry, and enjoy an excellent reputation at home and abroad. They form a strong backbone for Furniture China, and have inspired exhibitors to expand beyond merely exhibiting products to showcasing full-on interior spaces. Since being established, the Gold Idea Award has had 1,191 entries from 420 competing enterprises and is regarded as one of the most influential and high-profile awards within China's burgeoning furniture industry.

From Copying to Innovating

Since the 1990s, China's furniture industry has enjoyed a period of fast and comprehensive development, and over that time it has constantly striven to transition from 'Made in China' to 'Innovated in China'. That goal has undoubtedly been furthered by Furniture China, which continues to play a vital role in supporting and promoting the country's furniture industry, while encouraging it to move away from a 'copy + manufacture' model towards a more enlightened 'design + innovation' approach.

At present in China, original design is growing fast, with real innovation going from strength to strength. This has done a great deal to overcome the deep-rooted prejudice among overseas buyers that Chinese-made furniture is cheap, inferior and copyist. They now clearly see that China is producing furniture to the highest international standards. Meanwhile, among high-earning Chinese families, aesthetic standards in home decor are undergoing radical change, with 'European styles' gradually declining in popularity and original Chinese furniture being increasingly admired. This change of taste reflects a recovery of self-confidence in traditional culture. Indeed, traditional architecture and furniture, as well as cultural symbols with Chinese elements, have all been reinvigorated within the context of New Chinese Design.

It is clear that the stage is set for many new Chinese design brands to come to the fore, and equally clear that they do not feel tied to producing pieces that incorporate 'old-style' Chinese decoration and carving. They favour a simpler, more abstract style, a modern interpretation of traditional Chinese furniture that is on the way to becoming a definable furniture style in its own right.

Today, China has one of the most innovative furniture cultures in the world. Its original furniture design stands proudly on the world design stage and is held in high esteem internationally. Nonetheless, it is still in the early stages of development. Maybe in 10 or even 20 years China will become internationally recognised as a powerhouse of pioneering furniture design, manufacture and branding, but until then it will no doubt continue to thrill us with its bold ideas and inventiveness. We look forward to charting its progress, along with the growth of China's International Furniture Expo, in future editions of this book.

↓
Two exhibitor stands at
Furniture China, 2018

INDEX

Main entries are indicated in **bold**
Images in *italic* on page image appears

PICTURE CREDITS

Laurence King Publishing would like to thank the copyright holders for granting permission to reproduce works illustrated in this book. Every effort has been made to contact the holders of copyright material, and any omission will be corrected in future editions if the publisher is notified in writing.

All furniture designs and photographs are copyright the designers and design studios listed on page.

Key
a: above, **b:** below, **t:** top, **l:** left, **r:** right

11t Heritage Image Partnership Ltd/ Alamy; **13** Philadelphia Museum of Art, Purchased with the J. Stogdell Stokes Fund, the John T. Morris Fund, the Thomas Skelton Harrison Fund, the George W. B. Taylor Fund, and with funds contributed by Mr. and Mrs. Howard Lewis and Henry B. Keep, 1971-12-1; **14l** Philadelphia Museum of Art, Purchased with the Thomas Skelton Harrison Fund, 1967-141-1; **14r** Philadelphia Museum of Art, Purchased with Museum funds, 1929-91-5a; **15t** Philadelphia Museum of Art, 55¾ × 40½ × 18½ inches (141.6 × 102.9 × 47 cm) Purchased with Museum funds, 1959-117-4; **15b** Image courtesy of Channels Design.

ACKNOWLEDGEMENTS

What a wonderful, fascinating and extraordinary voyage of discovery this book project has been. Firstly, its succesful realization would not have been possible without the kind support of Wang Mingliang, founder of Furniture China Expo, who has offered countless insights and recommendations. Thanks must also go to Xu Xiangnan, President of China National Furniture Association, for his kind endorsement of the project. We would also like to thank Hou Zheng-Guang for not only introducing us to Mr Wang, but also penning such an interesting foreword and making so many useful suggestions along the way. Our deepest heartfelt thanks must go to our trusted co-editor and dear friend Zheng 'Jack' Qu, who has tirelessly and good-naturedly travelled with us on this remarkable design journey from the beginning, introducing us to people, places and things we would never have chanced upon ourselves. We are also hugely grateful to Jack's colleague Shirley Chen at the China Design Center, whose helpful input has been vital to the logistical co-ordination of this project. Likewise, we would like to thank Carrie Wang at Shanghai UBM SinoExpo for assisting us with invaluable research, too.

The team at Laurence King Publishing also deserve many thanks, especially: Jo Lightfoot for her editorial supervision of this project; Andrew Roff for his good-natured editorial management; Patricia Burgess and Robert Davies for their skilful copy-editing; Rosanna Fairhead for her thoughtful proofreading; Angus Hyland for his invaluable creative direction; Davina Cheung for overseeing its exacting production; Pauline Hubner for her careful indexing; and, last but by no means least, Alex Coco for his stunning graphic design work.

We would also like to thank all the many designers, design studios, gallery owners and manufacturers we have met on our travels who have so kindly hosted us, shared their stories, shown us their work, sent us imagery and information, and ultimately revealed to us their hopes and dreams for a new Chinese design renaissance. This is your remarkable design story, and we are eternally grateful to you for sharing it with us.

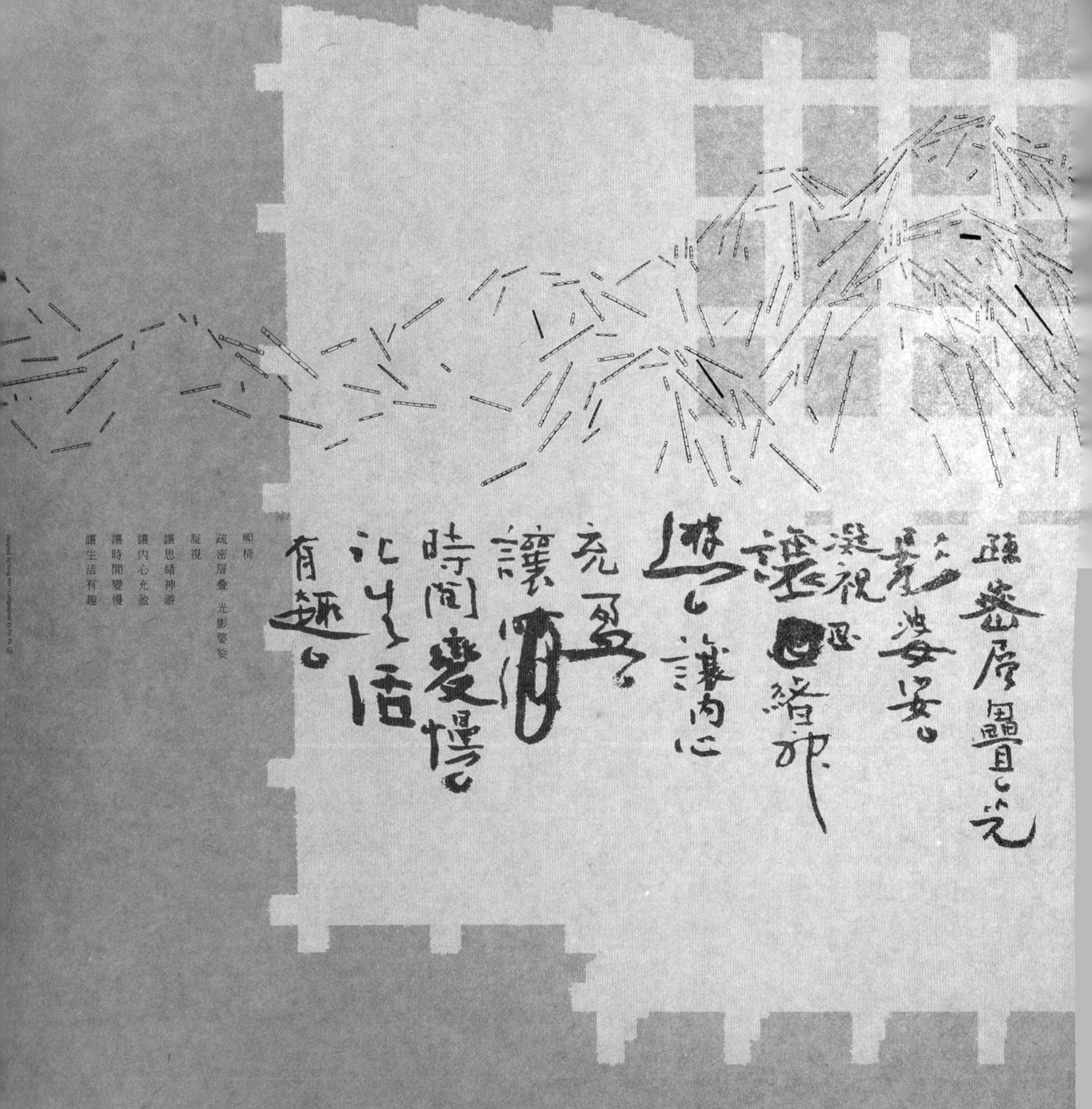

熙椅

疏密層疊 光影婆娑

凝視
讓思緒神游
讓內心充盈
讓時間變慢
讓生活有趣